Cambridge Direct Mathematics

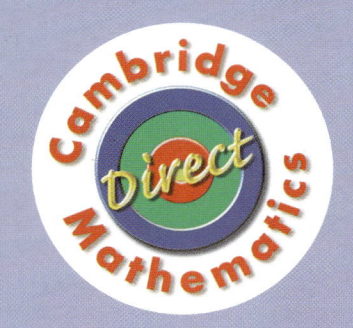

Measures, Shape, Space and Handling Data

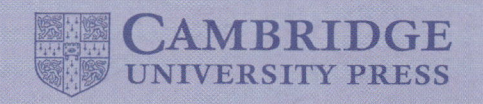

4

CAMBRIDGE UNIVERSITY PRESS

PUBLISHED BY THE PRESS SYNDICATE OF THE UNIVERSITY OF CAMBRIDGE
The Pitt Building, Trumpington Street, Cambridge, United Kingdom

CAMBRIDGE UNIVERSITY PRESS
The Edinburgh Building, Cambridge CB2 2RU, UK
40 West 20th Street, New York, NY 10011–4211, USA
10 Stamford Road, Oakleigh, VIC 3166, Australia
Ruiz de Alarcón 13, 28014 Madrid, Spain
Dock House, The Waterfront, Cape Town 8001, South Africa

http://www.cambridge.org

© Cambridge University Press 2001

First published 2001
Reprinted 2001

Printed in the United Kingdom at the University Press, Cambridge

Typefaces Frutiger, Sayer Script, Myriad, Helvetica, Comic Sans *System* QuarkXPress 4.03

A catalogue record for this book is available from the British Library

ISBN 0 521 78474 3 paperback

Text illustration by Adam Stower

General editors for Cambridge Mathematics Direct
Sandy Cowling, Jane Crowden, Andrew King, Jeanette Mumford

Writing team for *Measures, Shape, Space and Handling Data 4*
Ann Barber, Salliann Coleman, Pete Crawford, Jane Crowden, Sandy Cowling, Lorely James, Mary Nathan, Marian Reynolds, Elizabeth Toohig, Allison Toogood, Fay Turner, Joanne Woodward

The writers and publishers would like to thank the many schools and individuals
who trialled lessons for Cambridge Mathematics Direct.

NOTICE TO TEACHERS
It is illegal to reproduce any part of this work in material form (including photocopying and electronic storage) except under the following circumstances:
(i) where you are abiding by a licence granted to your school or institution by the Copyright Licensing Agency;
(ii) where no such licence exists, or where you wish to exceed the terms of a licence, and you have gained the written permission of Cambridge University Press;
(iii) where you are allowed to reproduce without permission under the provisions of Chapter 3 of the Copyright, Designs and Patents Act 1988.

Abbreviations and symbols
IP Interactive picture
CM Copymaster
A is practice work
B develops ideas
C is extension work
★ if needed, helps with work in A

A red margin indicates that activities are teacher-led.
A green margin indicates that activities are independent.

Contents

Measures (M)

M1	**Measuring length and perimeter**	
M1.1	Introducing perimeter	5
M1.4	Fractions and decimals of length measures	7
M1.5	Problems using measures of length	9
M2	**Measuring mass**	
M2.2	Adding and subtracting	11
M2.3	Halving and doubling	13
M2.4	Multiplying and dividing	15
M3	**Measuring capacity**	
M3.1	Reading scales	17
M3.2	Adding and subtracting litres and millilitres	18
M3.3	Halving and doubling litres and millilitres	20
M3.4	Multiplying litres and millilitres	22
M4	**Choosing and using measures**	
M4.1	Which unit?	24
M4.2	Using measuring equipment 1	26
M4.3	Using measuring equipment 2	27
M4.4	Solving problems with measures	28
M5	**Area and perimeter**	
M5.1	Finding perimeters	29
M5.3	Estimating area	31
M6	**Time**	
M6.1	Calendars and passing time	33
M6.3	Analogue clocks	35
M6.4	Linking digital and analogue time	37

Shape and space (SS)

SS1	**Naming, describing, classifying and making 2-D shapes**	
SS1.1	Describing 2-D shapes	38
SS1.2	Polygons	39
SS1.3	Making polygons	40

SS2	**Naming, describing, classifying and making 3-D shapes**	
SS2.1	Prisms	42
SS2.2	Polyhedra	43
SS2.3	Nets of 3-D shapes	44
SS2.4	Visualising shapes	45
SS3	**Naming, describing, classifying and making 2-D and 3-D shapes**	
SS3.1	Classifying and sorting 2-D and 3-D shapes	47
SS3.2	Investigating shapes	49
SS5	**Position and direction**	
SS5.1	Position and co-ordinates	50
SS5.2	Using co-ordinates	51
SS5.3	Describing and following directions	52
SS6	**Movement and angle**	
SS6.1	Measuring angles in degrees	54
SS6.4	Making and measuring turns	56

Handling data (HD)

HD1	**Using tally charts, frequency tables and pictograms**	
HD1.1	Tallying	57
HD1.2	Making pictograms	58
HD1.3	Using charts and tables	59
HD2	**Using bar charts**	
HD2.1	Reading bar charts	62
HD2.3	Interpreting bar charts	64
HD3	**Venn and Carroll diagrams**	
HD3.1	Venn diagrams	67
HD3.2	Carroll diagrams	70
HD3.3	Interpreting sorting diagrams	71

M1.1 Introducing perimeter

> **Key idea** — We measure the edges of a shape to find its perimeter.

★1 Find the perimeter of these shapes.

a

b

c

d

e

M1 Measuring length and perimeter

A1 Find the perimeter of these shapes.

Round your measurements to the nearest half-centimetre.

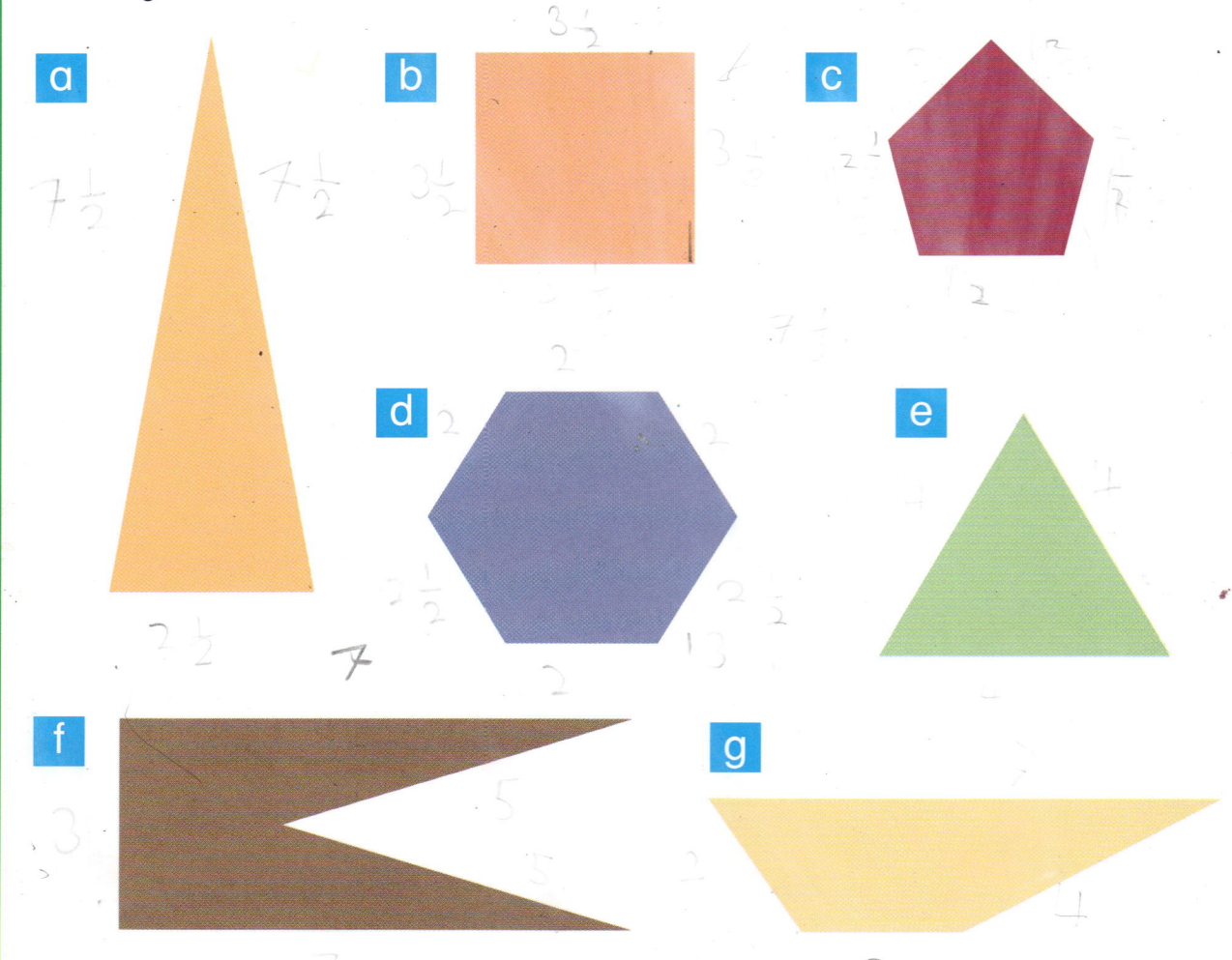

a

b

c

d

e

f

g

B1
 a Find a small object in the classroom.
    Draw around it in your book with a pencil.

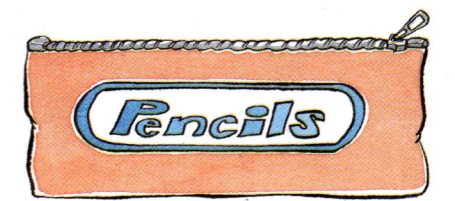

 b Estimate the perimeter in centimetres and half-centimetres.

 c How long is the perimeter to the nearest half-centimetre?

B2 Find the perimeter of 2 more small objects in the classroom.

Key idea We measure the edges of a shape to find its perimeter.

M1.4 Fractions and decimals of length measures

Key idea: There are 500 m in $\frac{1}{2}$ km and 50 cm in $\frac{1}{2}$ m.

Mrs Bows' ribbon shop

A1 Mrs Bows only has a centimetre measuring tape.

She has been asked for these lengths of ribbon in metres.

Can you convert these lengths into centimetres for her?

a $\frac{1}{2}$ m
b 1·70 m
c 1·68 m
d $\frac{1}{4}$ m
e 1·34 m
f 0·45 m
g 0·85 m
h $\frac{3}{4}$ m
i $1\frac{1}{4}$ m
j $1\frac{1}{2}$ m

A2 What metric units should Mrs Bows use to measure these?

a her journey home
b her thimble
c her curtains
d her pins
e her scissors
f her knitting needles

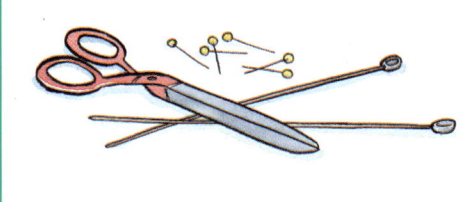

M1 Measuring length and perimeter

7

The sponsored walk

B1 The sponsored walk was measured in kilometres.

Work out how many metres each child walked.

Abigail 3.5 km

Keisha 2¾ km

Oliver 1¼ km

Mark 4.75 km

Emma 5½ km

Ruben 5.08 km

Andrew 4.20 km

Megan 3¼ km

Beth 2½ km

Sam 1¾ km

B2 Round each of your distances to the nearest 100 metres.

C1 You need cards from CM 4 and a partner.

Play 'Fraction pairs':

Lay the cards face down.

Take it in turns to turn over 2 cards.

If they match, you win the cards.

If they do not match turn the cards face down again.

The winner is the player with the most pairs of cards.

| Key idea | There are 500 m in ½ km and 50 cm in ½ m. |

M1 Measuring length and perimeter

M1.5 Problems using measures of length

| Key idea | We can use what we know about numbers and measures to solve problems. |

A1 Aruna's mother is making her a table to keep her school things on.

Aruna wants to put her things on it without any of them overlapping.

She says the table must be oblong in shape.

Here are Aruna's school things:

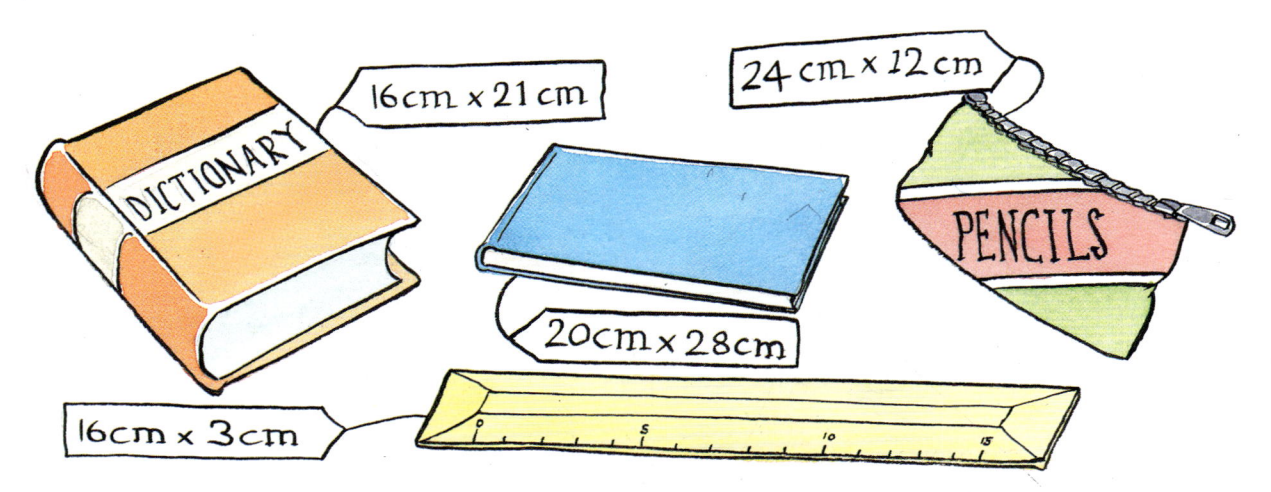

- Dictionary: 16 cm × 21 cm
- 20 cm × 28 cm
- Pencils: 24 cm × 12 cm
- 16 cm × 3 cm

What is the length and width of the smallest table her mother could make?

A2 When it is finished Aruna says she is going to stick a piece of red ribbon all around the edge of the table.

How much ribbon will she need?

B1 Aruna's twin sister Sheena wants a table but says it must be square. She has exactly the same things as Aruna.

a What size table should her mother make for Sheena?

b How much ribbon does she need?

B2 Can you suggest a sensible height for both tables?

M1 Measuring length and perimeter

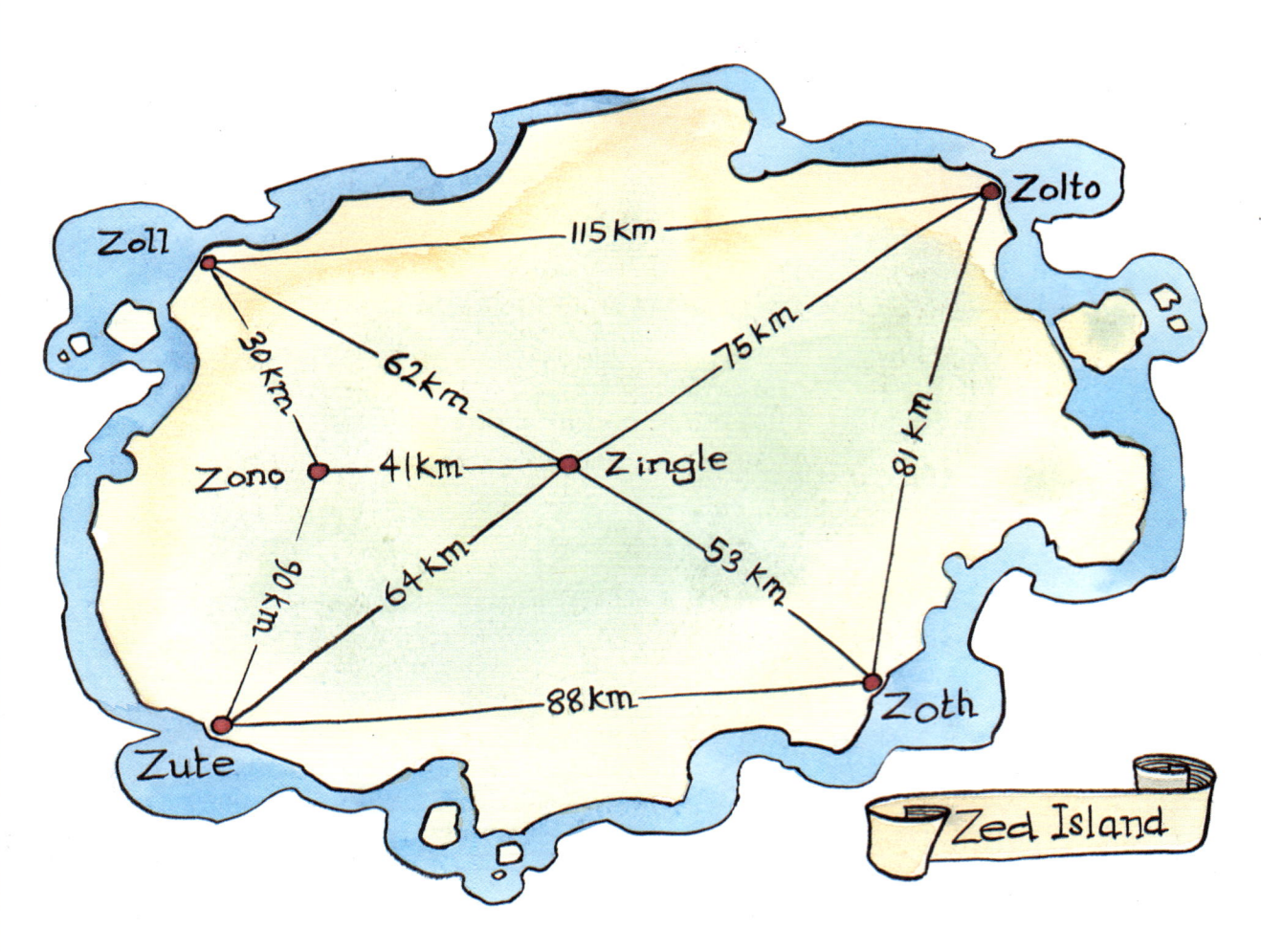

The map shows towns on Zed Island.

C1 **a** Which two towns are furthest apart?

b Which two towns are nearest each other?

C2 You need to visit all the towns. You must start and finish at Zute.

a What route would you take?

b How far would you have travelled?

Try and find the shortest route.

C3 Plan your own journeys, visiting 4 towns only.

Find the total distance travelled on each journey.

Key idea | We can use what we know about numbers and measures to solve problems.

10   M1 Measuring length and perimeter

M2.2 Adding and subtracting

> **Key idea** We can use what we know already to solve problems.

A1 Find the totals. Write a number sentence for each one.

a) 500 g + 200 g + 200 g
b) 200 g + 200 g + 50 g
c) 200 g + 100 g + 50 g
d) 200 g + 200 g + 200 g + 50 g

A2 Solve these problems.

Write a number sentence to explain how you did each one.

a) 2 cans of beans fill the saucepan.

One can holds 400 g of beans and he other 250 g.

Find the total mass in the saucepan.

b) Katie is making a cake.

She needs 350 g of flour.

There is only 100 g left.

How much more does she need?

c) Robert opened a 1 kg bag of sugar.

He poured 200 g into the sugar bowl.

How much was left in the bag?

M2 Measuring mass

B1 Sara needed 750 g of potatoes to make her soup.

She had 3 potatoes.

One weighed 250 g, one weighed 150 g and the third weighed 300 g.

Did she have enough potatoes?

Write a number sentence to explain your answer.

B2 Use some or all of these masses.

Make these totals.

Write a number sentence for each one.

a 600 g = 500 g + ☐

b 550 g   c 850 g   d 800 g

C1

a Find 10 weights that you could measure using some or all of these masses.

b What is the difference between the greatest and smallest weights you can measure?

c Find a multiple of 50 g that is less than 800 g but will not balance using these masses.

C2 Hassan is making bread. He needs to measure 400 g of flour with the balance scales and masses in C1.

How can he do it? Write a number sentence.

> **Key idea** We can use what we know already to solve problems.

12 M2 Measuring mass

M2.3 Halving and doubling

Key idea | We can use what we know about halving and doubling to solve problems.

★1 You need   4 × 100g   2 × 50g   6 × 10g   10 × 5g

Use them to help you do A1 and A2.

For example
Self-raising flour   100g + 100g   double →   100g 100g + 100g 100g

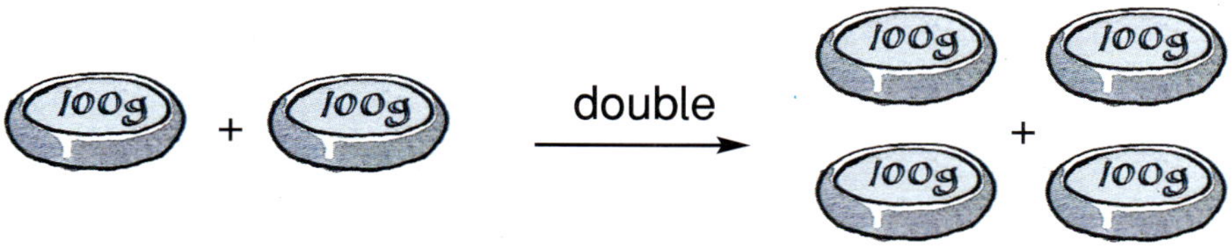

A1 Mrs Baker has a list of what she needs to make 12 rock cakes.

Ingredients:
200g self-raising flour
100g margarine
120g caster sugar
50g sultanas
25g cherries
30g currants
1 egg
2 tablespoons of milk

She needs to make more than 12 cakes.

a Double the amounts for her.
   Write a new list.

b How many rock cakes can she make now?

M2 Measuring mass

A2 Here is a recipe for 30 chocolate crispies.

CHOCOLATE CRISPIES
200g plain chocolate
50g margarine
250g cereal flakes
100g honey

Melt the honey, chocolate and margarine together. Stir in the cereal flakes and mix thoroughly until all the flakes are coated with chocolate mixture. Spoon into cake cases and leave to cool.

I only need to make 15.
How much of each ingredient should I use?

B1

a Add $\frac{1}{2}$ kg to 400 g. How many grams altogether?

b Double $\frac{3}{4}$ kg. How many grams?

c Add $\frac{1}{2}$ kg to $\frac{3}{4}$ kg. How many grams?

d How much more is $\frac{1}{2}$ kg than $\frac{1}{10}$ kg?

e What is half of

500 g? $\frac{1}{10}$ kg?   3 kg?

C1 Work with a partner.

You need only one 100 g mass, a set of balance scales, 3 containers and some sand.

Take it in turns to measure the following quantities of sand.

Put each into a separate container.

a 200 g   b 50 g   c 450 g

When you have finished, ask your partner to check how accurately you have measured.

You can check by using other masses on the balance or a kitchen scale with a numbered dial.

Key idea	We can use what we know about halving and doubling to solve problems.

M2 Measuring mass

M2.4 Multiplying and dividing

Key idea | We can use what we know about multiplication and division to solve problems.

★1 Look on the board at the list of amounts you need to make cheese straws.

Write a list to make twice as many.

You could use 100 g, 50 g, 10 g and 5 g masses to help you.

A1 To make these you need:

100 grams plain flour
5 grams bicarbonate of soda
10 grams ground ginger
25 grams margarine
50 grams soft brown sugar
20 grams golden syrup
enough milk to mix to a firm dough

Can you write the ingredients needed to make 30 gingerbread people?

B1 Work with a partner. You need:

Use just one 50 g mass and a set of balance scales.

Measure the following quantities of sand and put each into a separate container:

a 200 g   **b** 150 g   **c** 300 g

Make a note of how you managed to weigh out each quantity.

Write a number sentence to show how many lots of 50 g you used each time.

When you have weighed out all three amounts, check how accurately you have measured them by weighing them on a set of kitchen scales with a numbered dial.

M2 Measuring mass

C1 Sally, the Italian cook, needs to multiply
these amounts of pasta by 6.

a 25 g   b 150 g

c 500 g   d $\frac{1}{4}$ kg

What are the new amounts in grams?

She needs to multiply these amounts by 7.

e 30 g   f 200 g

g $\frac{1}{2}$ kg   h $\frac{1}{10}$ kg

What are the new amounts in grams?

C2 How many 200 g masses would you need
to balance 8 grapefruit weighing about 250 g each?

Explain how you worked out your answer.

C3 Three 'fun-size' chocolate bars weigh 50 g.
How many bars would you get in a 450 g pack?

C4 I have 5 oranges weighing 1 kg, and 4 apples weighing 600 g.

Which is heavier, an apple or an orange?

How much heavier?

> **Key idea** We can use what we know about multiplication and division to solve problems.

M3.1 Reading scales

> **Key idea** We need to look at the numbers above and below the level of the liquid to read the scale.

A1 How much liquid is in each container?

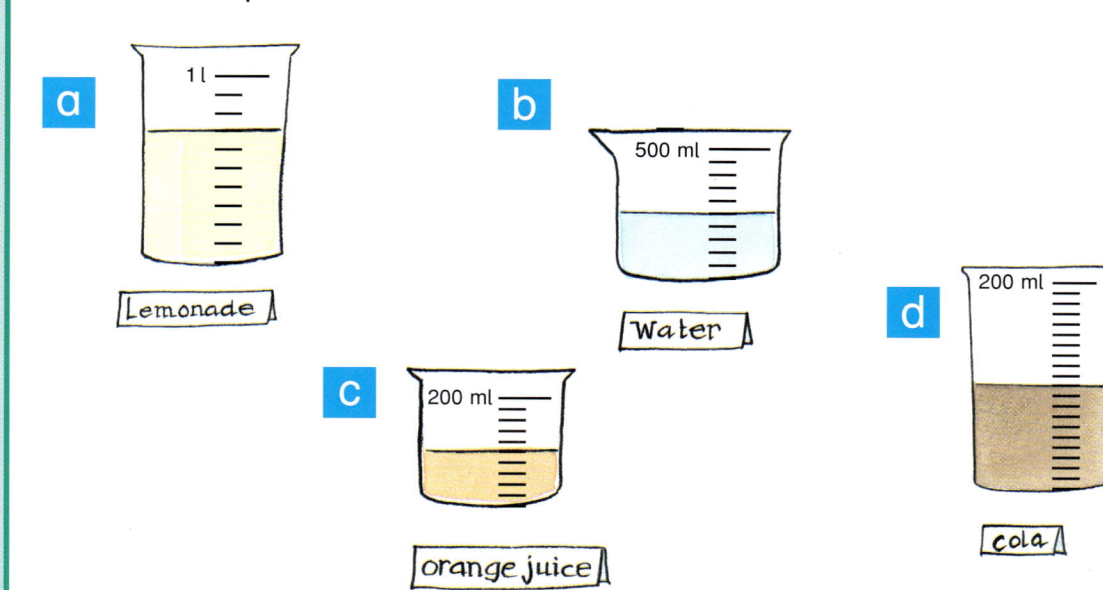

a Lemonade (1 l scale)

b Water (500 ml scale)

c orange juice (200 ml scale)

d cola (200 ml scale)

B1 You need CM 11.

Draw these levels on the measuring cylinders.

a $\frac{1}{4}$ l

b $\frac{1}{10}$ l

c $\frac{3}{4}$ l

d about a pint

C1 You need CM 11

The liquid in each container in A1 is poured into a litre measuring cylinder.

At the same time, some liquid is added or lost.

Draw the new level of each liquid on CM 11.

a 100 ml of lemonade is added.

b 70 ml of water is poured away.

c $\frac{1}{10}$ l of orange juice is drunk.

d $\frac{1}{4}$ l of cola is spilt.

M3 Measuring capacity

M3.2 Adding and subtracting litres and millilitres

> **Key idea** We can use what we know about adding and subtracting to solve problems involving litres and millilitres.

★1 Copy and complete.

a) 400 ml + 300 ml = ☐
b) 10 l + 15 l = ☐
c) 850 ml − 250 ml = ☐
d) 100 l − 5 l = ☐
e) 63 ml + 37 ml = ☐
f) $4\frac{3}{4}$ l − $1\frac{1}{2}$ l = ☐

B1 Round these measurements to the nearest 100 ml.

a) 769 ml
b) 431 ml
c) 857 ml
d) 614 ml

B2 How much is in each container to the nearest 10 ml?

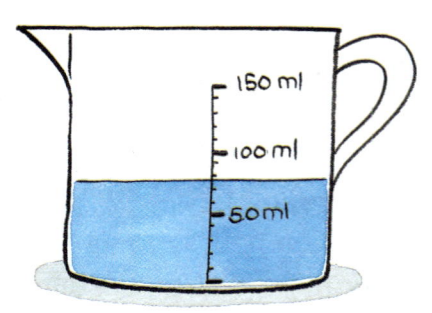

a) (jug showing liquid between 100 ml and 150 ml)

b) (jug showing liquid around 50–100 ml)

B3 a) Tommy needs 500 ml of milk to make pancakes.

The carton holds 800 ml of milk.

How much milk would be left when he has made the pancakes?

18   M3 Measuring capacity

b This morning there was 950 ml of lemonade in the jug.

The twins have drunk some and now there is only 600 ml left.

How much did they drink?

c Jamie's bucket holds $5\frac{1}{2}$ l and Jon's holds 7 l.

What is the total capacity of the two buckets?

d Mrs Turner has 15 l of petrol in her car.

The tank holds 60 l.

How much petrol does she need to buy to fill the tank?

Work out the answer too.

C1 Make up a word problem to fit each of the calculations in ★1.

| Key idea | We can use what we know about adding and subtracting to solve problems involving litres and millilitres. |

M3 Measuring capacity

19

M3.3 Halving and doubling litres and millilitres

Key idea | We can use what we know about halving and doubling to solve problems involving litres and millilitres.

Each of these recipes will make enough for 6 glasses of drink.

a Blackcurrant bomb

$\frac{1}{10}$ l blackcurrant cordial
$\frac{1}{2}$ l apple juice
400 ml water

b Homemade lemonade

1 l boiling water
2 oranges cut in quarters
4 lemons cut in quarters
$\frac{1}{2}$ l sugar syrup

c Tangy punch

$\frac{1}{10}$ l Lime cordial
50 ml lemon juice
500 ml grapefruit juice
$\frac{2}{10}$ l tonic water

d Chocolate-mint dream

200 ml chocolate syrup
$\frac{3}{4}$ l milk
300 ml cream
50 ml mint essence

M3 Measuring capacity

A1 There are 12 children at Jayne's party.

Everyone wants 1 glass of each drink.

Work out how much of each ingredient she will need for each drink.

B1 Nathan wants to make drinks for himself and his two brothers.

Work out how much of each ingredient he will need to make each drink.

B2 How much would Nathan need of each ingredient to make enough for 15 people?

Write your answers in
l and ml,
e.g. 1 l and 200 ml

| Key idea | We can use what we know about halving and doubling to solve problems involving litres and millilitres. |

M3 Measuring capacity

M3.4 Multiplying litres and millilitres

Key idea | We can use what we know about multiplication and division to solve problems involving litres and millilitres.

A1

a How much cola do you need to fill three 200 ml cups?

b How many 250 ml glasses can be filled from a 2-litre box of orange juice?

c How much water do you need to fill 4 bottles that each hold 150 ml?

d How many hot-water bottles that each need 1 l 500 ml can be filled from a 3-litre kettle?

e How much oil do you need for 5 bicycles if each bicycle needs 50 ml to oil its chain?

A2

a How many 175 ml coffee cups can you get out of a 1-litre coffee jug?

b How much water would you have left in a 2-litre jug after filling six 300 ml glasses?

c How much blackcurrant juice do you need to fill 4 flasks that each hold 340 ml?

d How much water would be left in a 5-litre drum after 3 people used 1500 ml of water each for washing?

e How many 15 ml spoons of medicine can you get out of a 200 ml bottle of medicine?

M3 Measuring capacity

C1

a How much water would be left in a 20-litre drinking trough after 8 horses had each drunk 2250 ml?

b Jamie, Dan, Tom and Sam each drank a 750 ml glass of milk out of a 4-litre container. How much milk was left?

c How many more 150 ml glasses of wine can you get from a 2-litre bottle than from a 750 ml bottle?

d Petrol leaks from a 2-litre can at a rate of 50 ml every day. How many weeks would it take for the can to empty?

e How many buckets does it take to fill a 25-litre paddling pool if each bucket holds 3 litres? How much water will be left in the last bucket?

| **Key idea** | We can use what we know about multiplication and division to solve problems involving litres and millilitres. |

M3 Measuring capacity

23

M4.1 Which unit?

| Key idea | We measure distances in kilometres or miles and capacity in litres or pints. |

You need the cards from CM 16 with 'pint' written on one blank card and 'mile' on the other.

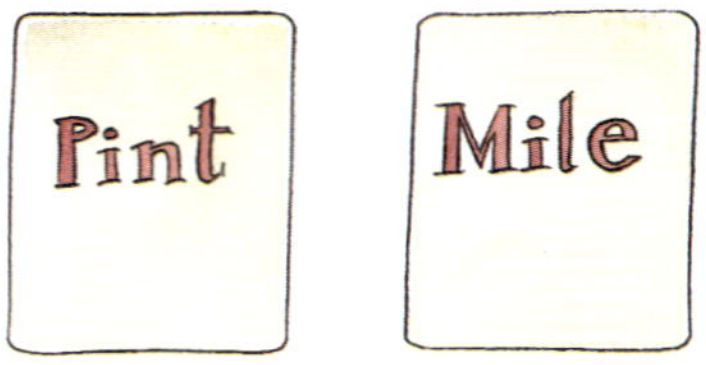

Pint   **Mile**

A1
- **a** Pick out all the units that measure length. Write them down.
- **b** Which of the length units is the largest?
- **c** Which of the length units is the smallest?
- **d** Write the length units in order, starting with the smallest.

A2 Pick out these cards: 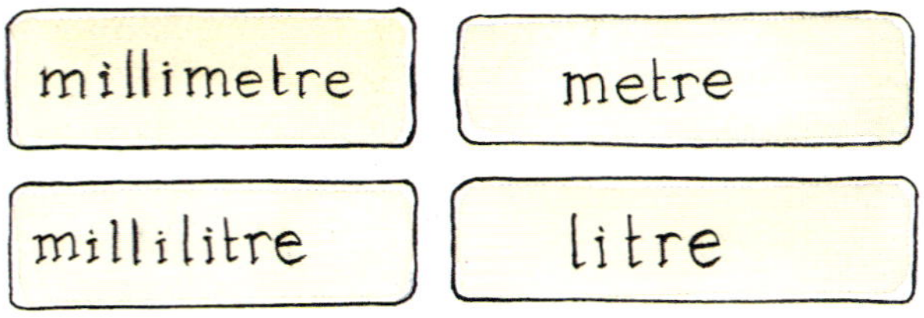
- **a** How many millimetres in a metre?
- **b** How many millilitres in a litre?
- **c** What do you think 'milli' means?

millimetre   **metre**
millilitre   **litre**

B1 What units are useful for measuring:
- **a** the weight of a feather? 
- **b** the weight of a bag of potatoes? 
- **c** the length of a bus? 
- **d** the thickness of a matchstick? 
- **e** the capacity of a tablespoon? 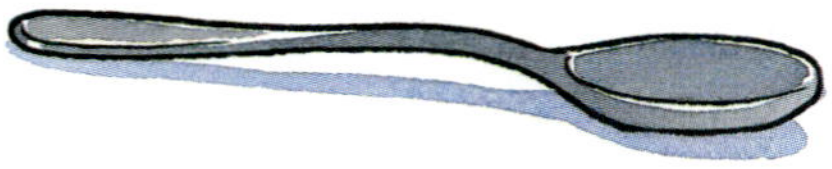
- **f** the distance between two places?

24   M4 Choosing and using measures   CM 16

B2 10 km is about the same distance as 6 miles.

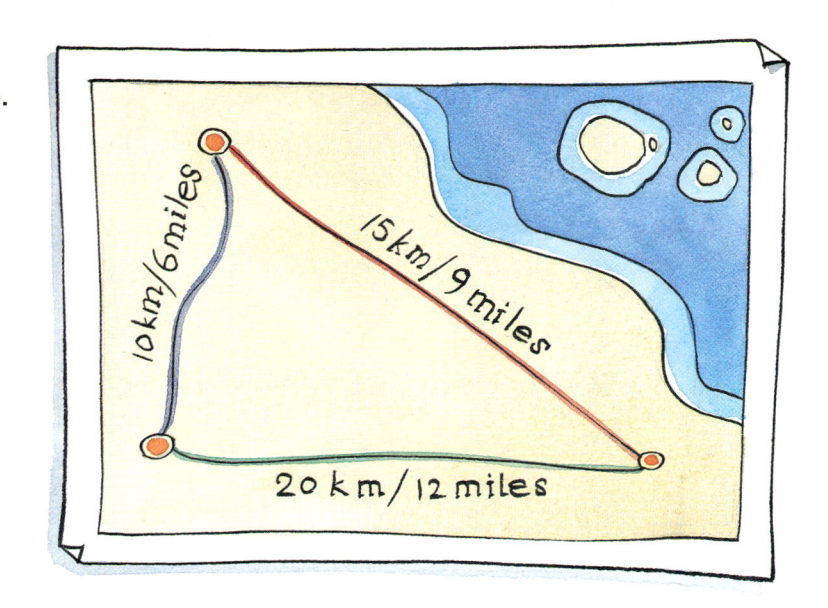

Look at the map.

Copy and complete this table.

kilometres	miles
10	6
15	
	12
25	
	18
35	

C1 Work in a group of 2 or 3.

You need a litre jug or bottle, a plastic pint glass and some large containers.

a Use the litre jug to measure the capacity of each container in litres.

Convert your measurements to pints.

Remember 1 litre is roughly 2 pints.

b Use a plastic pint glass to check your results.

Try and find a more accurate way to convert litres to pints.

Experiment with 1 litre, then 2 litres, then 3 litres ...

Key idea | We measure distances in kilometres or miles and capacity in litres or pints.

M4 Choosing and using measures

25

M4.2 Using measuring equipment 1

| Key idea | We need to choose the most useful equipment for whatever we are measuring. |

★1 Look at the pictures in A1.
Write down the nearest labelled measurement.

★2 Finish CM 17, rounding each measurement to the nearest 10 or 100.

A1 Write each measurement as accurately as possible. Look at the scales.

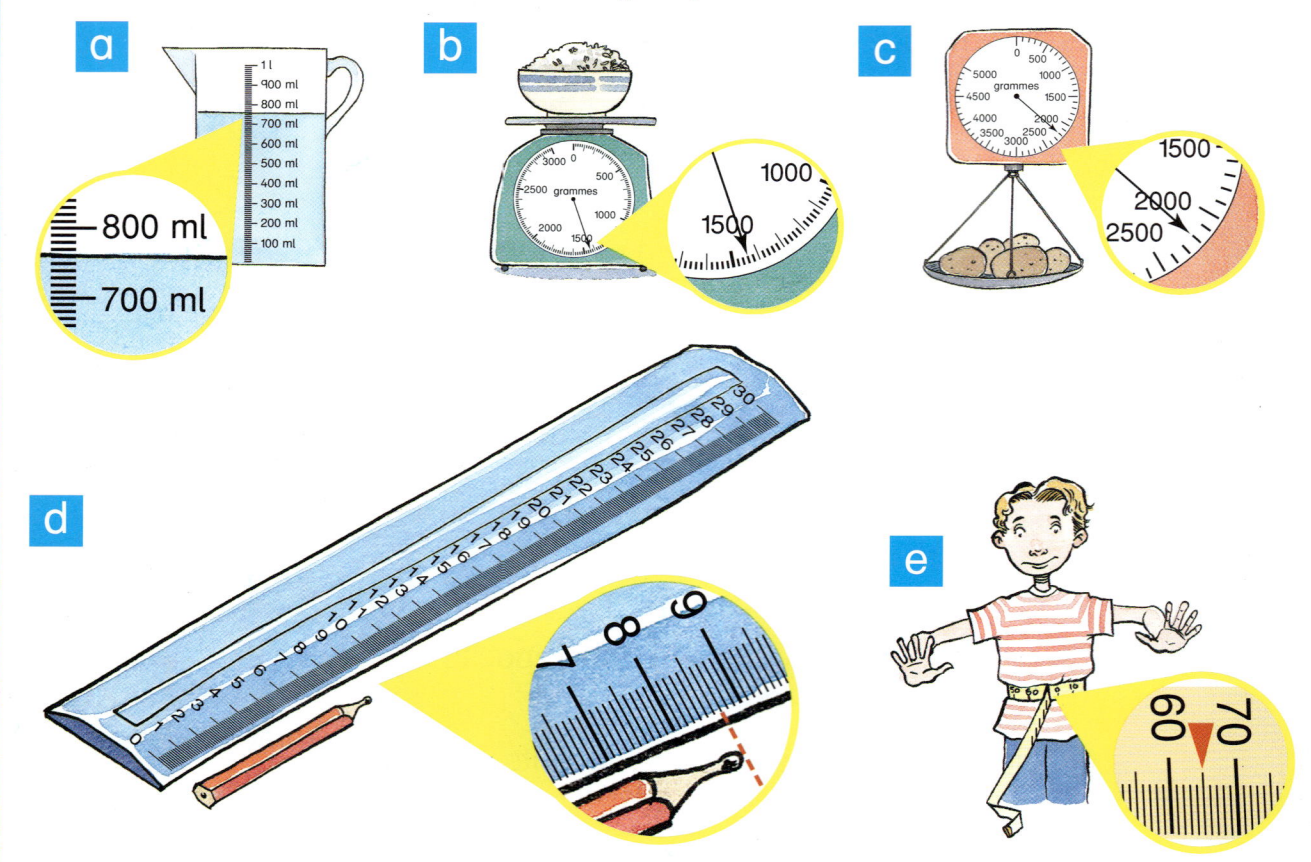

A2 Decide whether to round the measurements in A1 to the nearest 10 or 100 units.
Write down the rounded measurements.

A3 Finish CM 17, rounding each measurement to the nearest 10 or 100.

B1 a Do A1 and A2.   b Draw 3 pictures of measurements with scales.
Try and use g, ml and mm.
Write down each measurement.

C1 Invent some different scales for measuring length or mass.
Draw them accurately and try them out on a friend.
Can they read any measurement on the scale easily?

26   M4 Choosing and using measures

M4.3 Using measuring equipment 2

| Key idea | We need to choose the most useful equipment for whatever we are measuring. |

★1 Look at each picture in A1.
What equipment would you use to measure the length or height?

A1 Look at each picture.

Write what you could measure and what equipment you would use.

Find as many measurements as you can for each picture.

Example: The cat

I could measure
- its height with a ruler,
- its 'waist' with a tape measure,
- its weight with some bathroom scales.

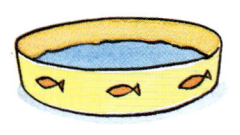

a
b
c
d
e
f
g
h

Pretend they are real.

B1 Do A1.

B2 Estimate one of the measurements you suggested for each picture in A1.

C1 Find out about how people make really large measurements.

Look at maths books or an encyclopaedia, or find information using a computer. Search under
- *measuring* • *surveying* • *maps*
- *space*

M4 Choosing and using measures

27

M4.4 Solving problems with measures

Key idea | We can use what we know about numbers to solve problems with measures.

A1 The trunk of a tree is 3 m high.
The branches go up another 6 m. How tall is the tree?

A2 Mrs James is making headbands for the school play.
Each child needs 50 cm of material.
How much material does she need for 4 children?

A3 Beth bought 80 g of toffees. She ate 35 g. How much was left?

A4 How many children can have 500 ml glasses of cola from a 2 l bottle?

B1 Jamie has a 60 cm long piece of wood.
He wants to cut it into 4 equal pieces to make a square frame.
How long should he make each piece?

B2 The head teacher wants to put a new fence around the school field.
The field is a rectangle that is 60 m long and 35 m wide.
How much fencing is needed to go all the way round the field?

B3 Zak is trying to make the scales balance.
He has a $\frac{1}{2}$ kg mass on one side and a 350 g can of beans on the other.
How many 10 g masses must he add to the can of beans to make it balance?

C1 Jade has 100 ml and 500 ml containers and a large bucket of unknown capacity.
She needs to mix some car shampoo with 1200 ml of water.
Explain how she can measure the water.

C2 A pound coin is 3 mm thick.
Tom is trying to fill a tube 9 cm tall.
So far he has collected 25 coins.
How many more will fill the tube?

M4 Choosing and using measures

M5.1 Finding perimeters

> **Key idea** | The perimeter of a flat shape is the distance around its edges.

A1 You need a ruler and a metre stick.

Find the perimeter of:

- **a** the top of your table,
- **b** your reading book,
- **c** the board.

A2 Find the perimeter of these rectangles.

- **a** long side 3 cm, short side 1 cm
- **b** long side 10 cm, short side 7 cm
- **c** long side 18 cm, short side 13 cm
- **d** long side 4 m, short side 50 cm

A3 A rectangle has a perimeter of 20 cm.

Draw 2 different rectangles with this perimeter.

B1
- **a** The length of a square tile is 20 cm.

  What is the perimeter?

- **b** Find a quick way to work out the perimeter of a square if you know the length of one side.

M5 Area and perimeter

B2 These ponds are all regular shapes.

Calculate each perimeter.

a 3 m, 3 m, 3 m, 3 m, 3 m (pentagon)

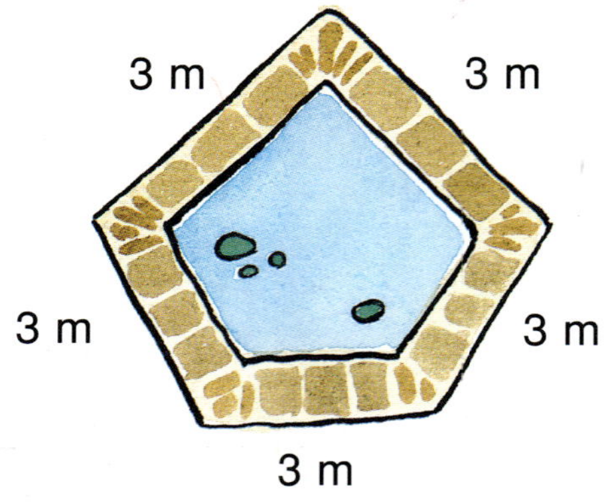

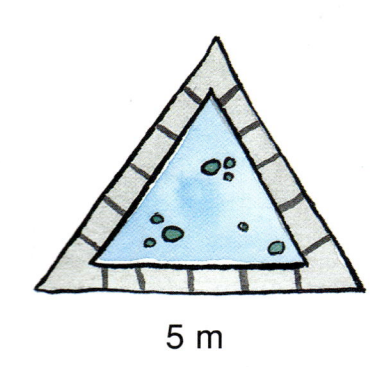

b 5 m (triangle)

c 2 m (hexagon)

B3 Here are some perimeters of squares.

What is the length of each side?

a 40 cm **b** 32 cm **c** 36 cm

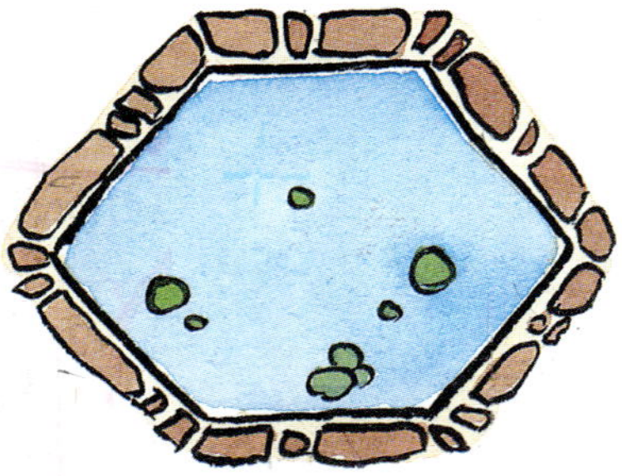

> A regular shape has sides of equal length.

Key idea The perimeter of a flat shape is the distance around its edges.

30   M5 Area and perimeter

M5.3 Estimating area

| Key idea | The area of something is the amount of surface it has. |

A1 Estimate the area of these shapes, then measure and check.

a

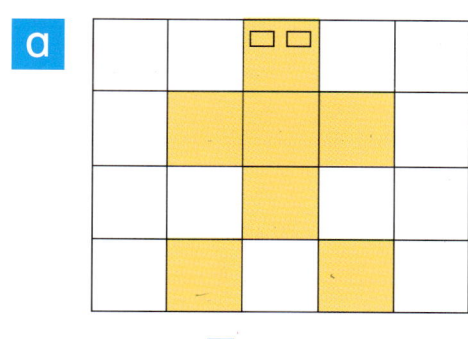

Estimate = ☐ square centimetres
Area = ☐ square centimetres

b

Estimate = ☐ square centimetres
Area = ☐ square centimetres

c

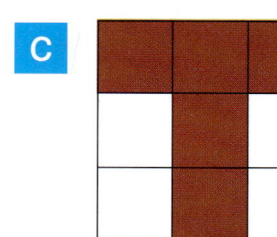

Estimate = ☐ square centimetres
Area = ☐ square centimetres

d

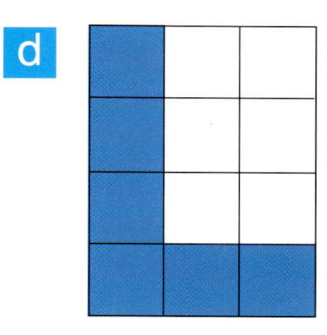

Estimate = ☐ square centimetres
Area = ☐ square centimetres

e

Estimate = ☐ square centimetres
Area = ☐ square centimetres

A2 Do CM 22.

B1 Write the area of these shapes. Don't forget to add half squares.

a

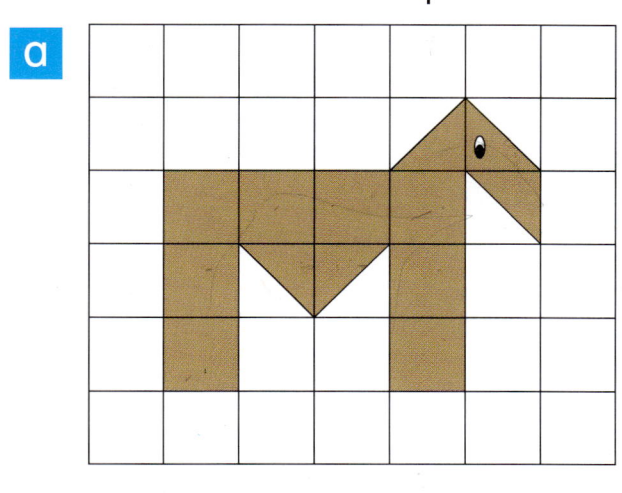

Estimate = ☐ square centimetres
Area = ☐ square centimetres

b

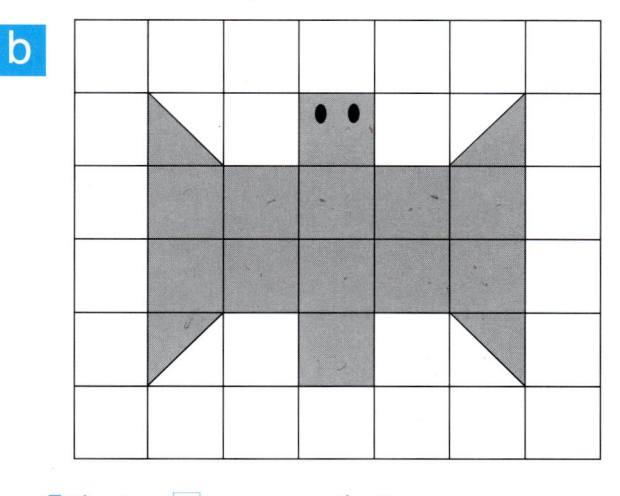

Estimate = ☐ square centimetres
Area = ☐ square centimetres

Turn over

M5 Area and perimeter

c

d

Estimate = ☐ square centimetres

Area = ☐ square centimetres

e

Estimate = ☐ square centimetres

Area = ☐ square centimetres

Estimate = ☐ square centimetres

Area = ☐ square centimetres

B2 Draw 3 letters from your name on squared paper and write the area.

C1 You need a pinboard and CM 23.

Find and draw different ways of halving the area of a 5 x 5 pinboard.

Example

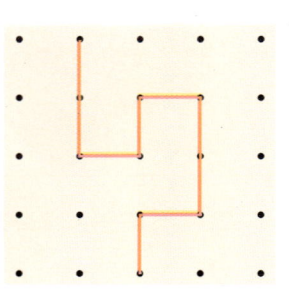

Key idea The area of something is the amount of surface it has.

32   M5 Area and perimeter

CM 23

M6.1 Calendars and passing time

| Key idea | We use a calendar to find out about dates, days, weeks, months and years. |

You need CM 25.

A1 Tom's birthday is 30 May.

Bob is exactly 6 weeks older than Tom. When is Bob's birthday?

A2 The summer term ends on 20 July.

The holiday lasts 6 weeks and 3 days.

When does school re-start?

A3

Pensbury Castle
Opening times

1 April to 1 October
daily
Early closing on
Sundays

a How many months is the castle open for?

b How many weeks is the castle open for?

c On how many days will the castle close early?

d Is the castle open on Saturday 16 June?

A4 **a** When do these plants begin to flower?

b When might the plants stop flowering?

Seeds
Flowering begins mid-May and lasts for 6-8 weeks

M6 Time

B1 You need CM 25.

Explorers are planning a trip up the Amazon to search for new plants.

They intend to start the expedition on 1 June.

Their planned schedule is:

2 weeks at base camp on the coast

2 weeks to buy equipment

3 weeks' canoe trip up river

4 weeks' stay in forest camp

3 weeks' return canoe trip to base camp

a When will they be back at base camp?

b When do they reach the forest camp?

c When do they leave the forest camp?

d Where are they on 16 July?

C1 You need CM 25.

Plan your own trip. Choose your starting place and your destination.

Write the times for all the activities.

a Where do you start your journey?

b Where are you going?

c How will you get there?

d How long will it take?

e When do you start?

f When do you return?

g Make up 3 questions about your trip.

Key idea We use a calendar to find out about dates, days, weeks, months and years.

M6 Time

M6.3 Analogue clocks

> **Key idea**: When the minute hand is between o'clock and half past, we say minutes past the last hour. When the minute hand is between half past and o'clock, we say minutes to the next hour.

A1 The Fun Bus visits all the town's leisure attractions, taking 20 minutes between each stop.

Copy and complete the timetable.

	Bus 1	Bus 2	Bus 3
Town Centre	20 past 10		
Water World			10 to 3
Sports Stadium			
Multi-screen Cinema		quarter to 1	
Bowling Alley			
Theme Park			

B1 Here is the programme for the school's summer fete.

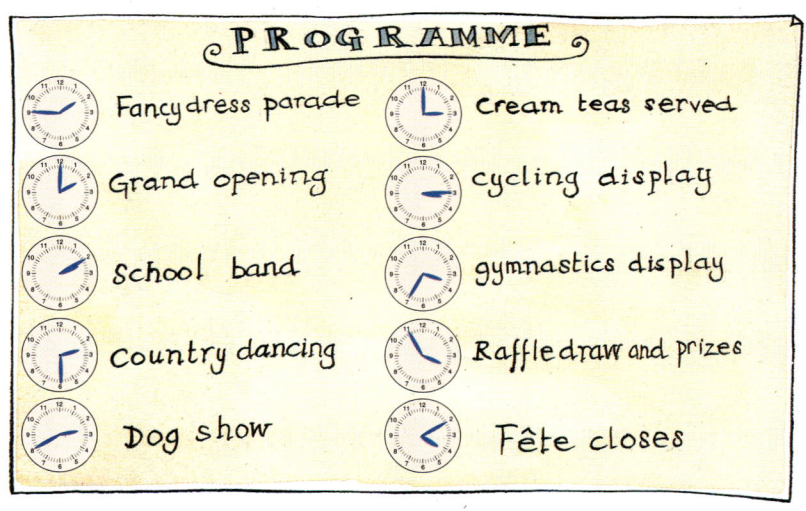

PROGRAMME
- Fancy dress parade
- Cream teas served
- Grand opening
- Cycling display
- School band
- Gymnastics display
- Country dancing
- Raffle draw and prizes
- Dog show
- Fête closes

a If you arrive at quarter past 3, how long must you wait for the Raffle Draw?

b How long does the Country Dancing take?

c It takes 50 minutes for Ajit and Robin to set up the Cream Teas.
What time do they begin?

d You have to finish your tea before the Raffle Draw.
How long do you have to eat it?

M6 Time

35

C1

MAGGY
20 past 2

INDIRA

HARRY

17 past 4
ED

For each child's clock or watch, write the times

a 5 minutes earlier,

b 3 minutes later,

c 7 minutes later,

d 11 minutes earlier.

Key idea When the minute hand is between o'clock and half past, we say minutes past the last hour. When the minute hand is between half past and o'clock, we say minutes to the next hour.

M6.4 Linking digital and analogue time

Key idea | Time can be shown and read in different ways.

TV Guide

A new channel 'Numeracy Fun' has just started.
Here is a typical day's programming.

Morning
9:00   Fun Facts and Figures
9:25   Daring Digits
10.05 Number Showtime
10:44 Numeracy News

Afternoon
12:00 Crazy Shapes
1:08   Helpline
1:20   Mega Measures
2:15   Fantastic Fractions
2:36   Problems Parade
4:05   Calculator Fun and Games
4:46   Singing Tables
5:30   News Round-up. Ends 6:00 p.m.

B1 How much television is shown in the morning?

B2 How much television is shown in the afternoon?

B3 Which is the longest programme in the morning?
How long does it last?

B4 Which is the shortest programme in the afternoon?
How long does it last?

B5 Choose 3 programmes you might watch and add their times together.

B6 Make up 2 questions of your own about the TV guide.
Ask a friend to answer them.

M6 Time

37

SS1.1 Describing 2-D shapes

> **Key idea**: Isosceles triangles have 2 sides of equal length.
> All sides are the same length in an equilateral triangle.

A1 You need scissors and glue.
Do CM 36.

B1 What is shown on each circle?

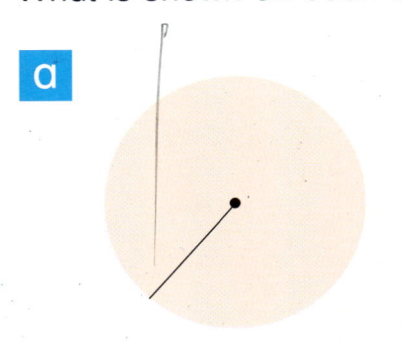

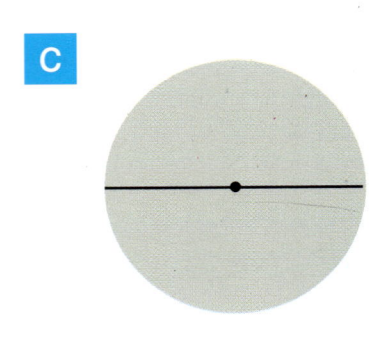

a   b   c

B2 Write a sentence about:

a the diameter of a circle,

b the radius of a circle.

You need equilateral and isosceles triangles.

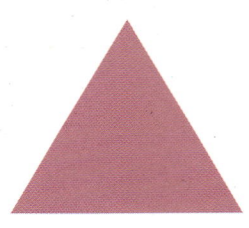

B3 a Can you draw a hexagon by drawing round an equilateral triangle?

b Can you draw a hexagon by drawing round an isosceles triangle?

B4 Draw a star by drawing round an

a equilateral triangle,   b isosceles triangle.

SS1 Naming, describing, classifying and making 2-D shapes

SS1.2 Polygons

> **Key idea** A polygon is a closed, flat shape with 3 or more straight sides.

A1 You need 6 flat shapes.

Sort the shapes into polygons and not-polygons.

a Draw round the 'polygons' in your book.
   Label them polygons.

b Draw round the shapes that are not polygons.
   Label them 'not-polygons'.

A2 Copy and complete this table.

Number of sides	Name of shape
7	heptagon
	pentagon
3	
	circle
	octagon
6	

C1 You need these regular shapes: triangle, square, pentagon, hexagon, heptagon, octagon.

a Draw round them.

b Compare the square's angles with the triangle's angles.
   What do you notice?

c Compare the angles inside all the polygons.
   What happens to the angles as the number of sides increases?

SS1 Naming, describing, classifying and making 2-D shapes

SS1.3 Making polygons

> **Key idea** | A polygon is a closed, flat shape with 3 or more straight sides.

You need a pinboard, rubber bands and CM 71.

★1
- a Make a triangle.
- b Draw it on CM 71.

★2
- a Make the largest triangle you can.
- b Draw it on CM 71.

★3
- a Make the smallest triangle you can.
- b Draw it on CM 71.

★4
- a Make as many more different triangles as you can.
- b Draw them on CM 71.

SS1 Naming, describing, classifying and making 2-D shapes

B1 You need paper, scissors and glue.

Fold a piece of paper in half.

Cut it so that when you open it up you have a hole that is

- **a** a quadrilateral,
- **b** a hexagon,
- **c** a triangle,
- **d** a square.

B2
- **a** Stick your shapes from B1 in your book.
- **b** Draw in the lines of symmetry.

B3 Do CM 38.

C1 You need a pinboard, rubber bands, a mirror and CM 71.

- **a** Make a square.
- **b** Draw it on CM 71.
- **c** Now make a square like this:
- **d** Draw it on CM 71.
- **e** How many squares can you see?
- **f** How many lines of symmetry does this shape have?
- **g** How many lines of symmetry does an undivided square have?

Key idea A polygon is a closed, flat shape with 3 or more straight sides.

SS1 Naming, describing, classifying and making 2-D shapes

SS2.1 Prisms

> **Key idea** A prism has 2 identical end faces and the same cross-section throughout its length.

B1 Copy and complete this table:

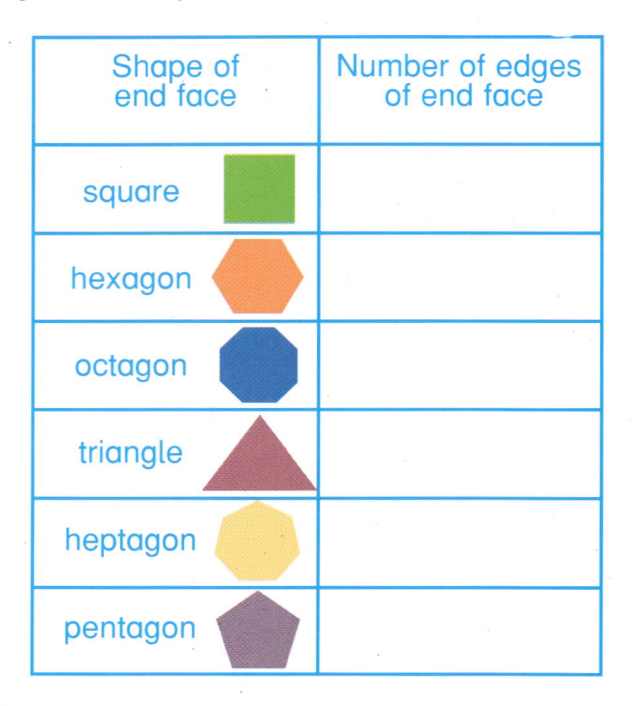

Shape of end face	Number of edges of end face
square	
hexagon	
octagon	
triangle	
heptagon	
pentagon	

B2 Draw and complete this table using your answers to B1.

Number of edges of end face	Number of faces altogether in the prism

B3 How many faces will a prism have if its end face has 23 edges?

C1 Draw and complete this table using your answers to B1.

Number of edges of end face	Number of edges altogether in the prism

C2 How many edges will a prism have if its end face has 17 edges?

C3 Investigate the number of edges of the end face and the number of vertices altogether.

SS2.2 Polyhedra

> **Key idea** — Each face of a polyhedron is a flat surface and is a polygon.

A1 You need dominoes from CM 39 and is a partner.

Play shape dominoes.
- Turn the dominoes upside down and take 7 each.
- Match dominoes that are similar but not identical.
- If you cannot go, take another domino.
- The first to play all their dominoes is the winner.

You can match a cylinder to a circle because a cylinder has circular ends.

A2 What are these shapes?

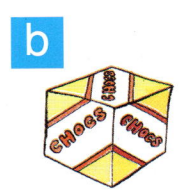

a b c d e

A3 Which of the shapes in A2 are polyhedra?

B1 You need a collection of 3-D shapes.

a Sort them into polyhedra and not-polyhedra. Draw and complete a table.

b Sort your shapes again. Cop and complete this table:

	polyhedra	not-polyhedra
4 or more vertices		
fewer than 4 vertices		

c Find 2 more ways to sort your shapes like this.

SS2 Naming, describing, classifying and making 3-D shapes

SS2.3 Nets of 3-D shapes

| Key idea | We can make a flat shape called a net by unfolding a hollow 3-D shape. |

B1 What 3-D shapes are these the nets for?

a

b

c

d

e

f

B2 How did you find the answers to B1?

SS2 Naming, describing, classifying and making 3-D shapes

SS2.4 Visualising shapes

Key idea | We can guess what a 3-D shape looks like on a side that is not facing us.

★ 1 You need 3-D shapes.

Make this robot.

SS2 Naming, describing, classifying and making 3-D shapes

45

A1 Look at the diagrams.

How many cubes do you need to make the shapes?

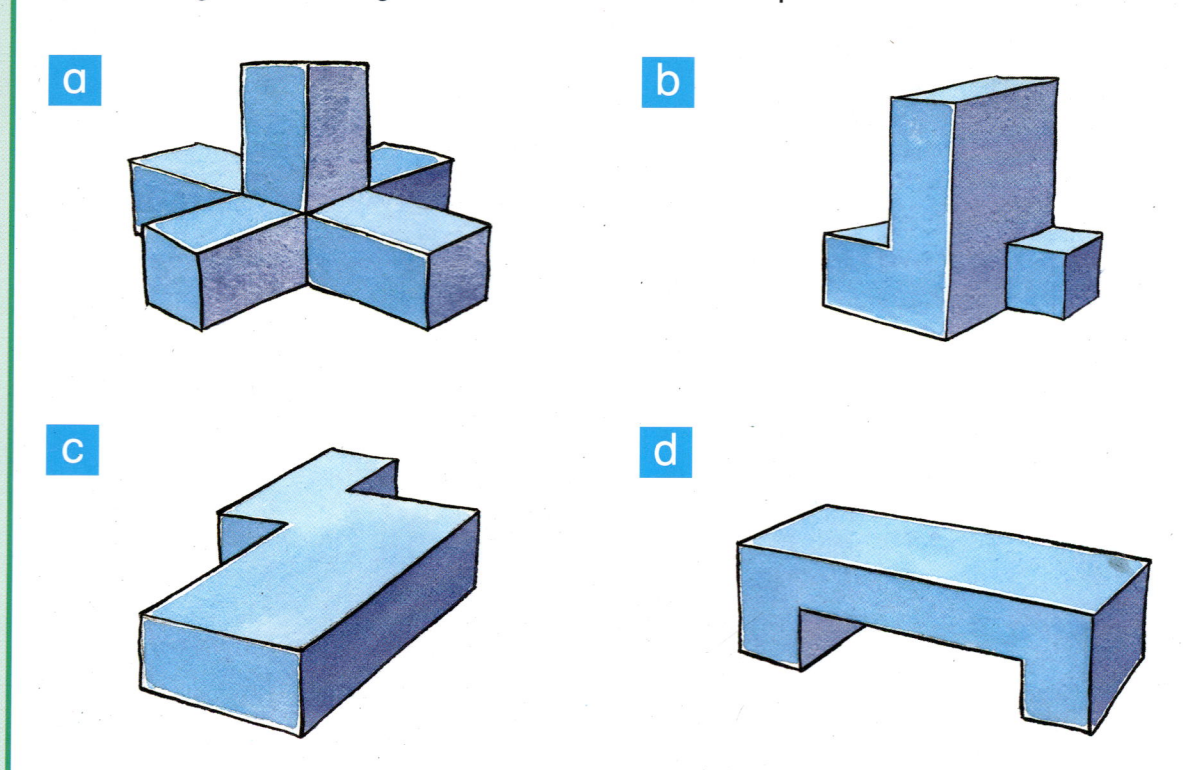

a

b

c

d

A2 You need Multilink cubes.

a Build the shapes in A1.

b How many cubes did you need for each shape?

C1 You need Multilink cubes.

This diagram is not very clear.

Make 3 different models that it might show.

| Key idea | We can guess what a 3-D shape looks like on a side that is not facing us. |

SS2 Naming, describing, classifying and making 3-D shapes

SS3.1 Classifying and sorting 2-D and 3-D shapes

> **Key idea** — We need to use the correct words to describe shapes.

★1 You need these shapes:

heptagon   rectangle
cylinder
cuboid
cone
hemi-sphere   cube

- **a** Use these shapes to make a tall model.
- **b** Use the shapes to make a short model.

A1 You need 2-D and 3-D shapes, and a partner.

- **a** Secretly build a model.

    Don't let your partner see it.

- **b** Describe your model for your partner to build.
- **c** Is their model the same as yours?

SS3 Naming, describing, classifying and making 2-D and 3-D shapes

C1 You need a mirror and 2-D shapes.

How many lines of symmetry do these shapes have?

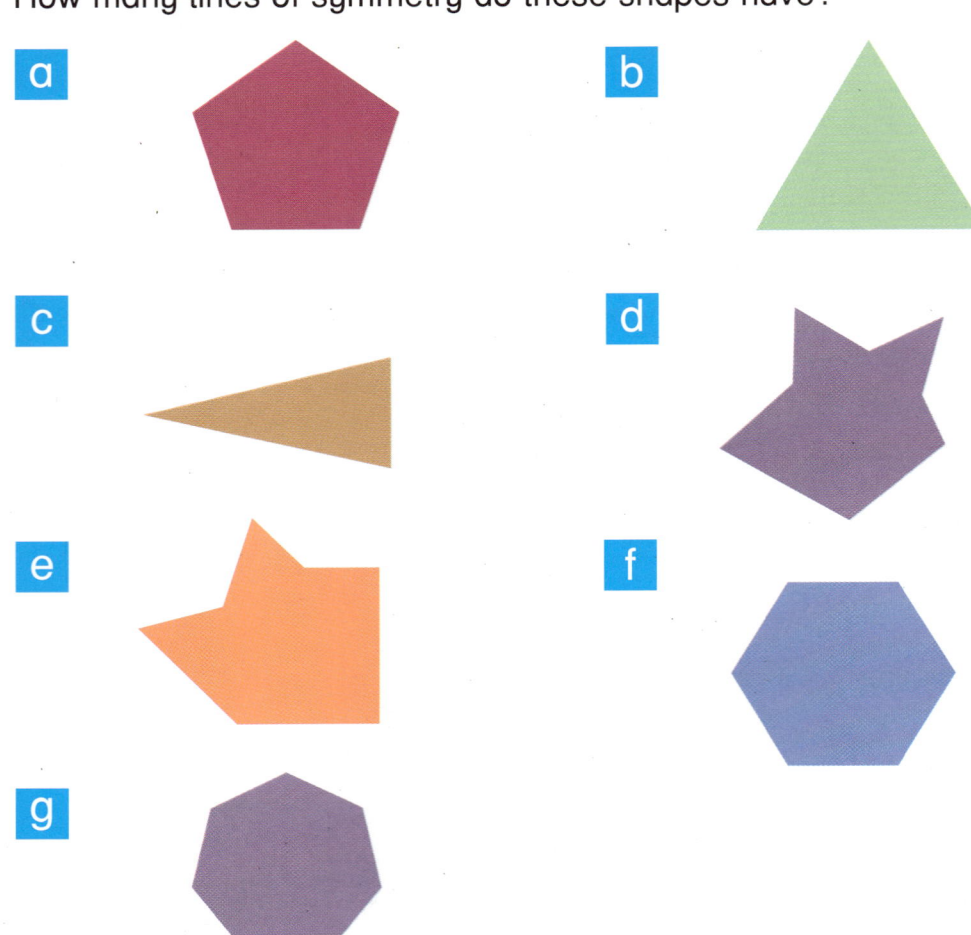

a

b

c

d

e

f

g

C2 Sort the shapes into 'have lines of symmetry' and 'have no lines of symmetry'.

C3 Write 3 sentences about lines of symmetry and 2-D shapes.

C4 How many lines of symmetry will a regular 10-sided shape have?

Key idea We need to use the correct words to describe shapes.

SS3 Naming, describing, classifying and making 2-D and 3-D shapes

SS3.2 Investigating shapes

Key idea	We can investigate shapes by looking at their properties.

A1 You need a partner.

- **a** Secretly draw a picture that uses 2-D shapes.

- **b** Describe your picture for your partner to draw but do **not** use any of the names of the shapes.
You can only describe them using the properties of the shapes!

- **c** Did your partner draw a picture that looks like yours?

B1 You need 2-D and 3-D shapes.

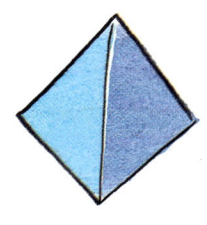

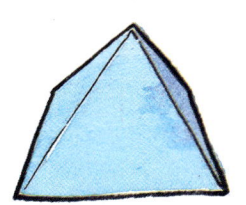

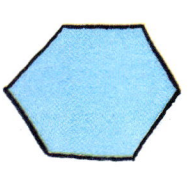

Find 5 examples to match each statement.

- **a** The number of vertices in a prism is a multiple of 2.

- **b** Pyramids have an even number of edges.

- **c** The number of lines of symmetry in a regular polygon is equal to the number of sides of the polygon.

B2 For each of the statements in B1, write 2 sentences explaining why it is true.

SS3 Naming, describing, classifying and making 2-D and 3-D shapes

SS5.1 Position and co-ordinates

> **Key idea** — We can describe a position on a grid by using 2 numbers.

You need CM 48.

A1 Look at the map of the pirate island.

Write what is at these points:

- **a** (8, 2)
- **b** (3, 2)
- **c** (7, 8)
- **d** (4, 8)
- **e** (5, 7)

(8, 2) means 8 across, then 2 up.

A2 Write what is at these points:

- **a** (1, 6)
- **b** (7, 6)
- **c** (6, 2)
- **d** (1, 8)
- **e** (9, 1)

B1 Use CM 48.

Draw
- **a** a pirate camp near Snake Swamp at (2, 3)
- **b** One-eye Jake's ship in Silver Bay at (2, 7)
- **c** another bridge over the river at (6, 8)

C1 Use CM 49.

- **a** Make your own map and label it. It doesn't have to be for pirates.
- **b** List everything on your map. Give the co-ordinates for each position.

SS5 Position and direction

SS5.2 Using co-ordinates

Key idea | We must remember to write the horizontal number first when we find the co-ordinates of a point on a grid.

A1 Look at the pirate island on IP 21 or CM 48.

Find the co-ordinates for these places.

- **a** Carib Village (4, ☐)
- **b** Pirate Camp (☐, 2)
- **c** Ashak Rainforest (☐, ☐)
- **d** Zantu Rainforest (☐, ☐)
- **e** Smugglers' Island (☐, ☐)
- **f** Galleon Lake (☐, ☐)
- **g** The Red Pig (☐, ☐)
- **h** Blue Mountain (☐, ☐)
- **i** Thunder Volcano (☐, ☐)
- **j** Hangman's Rock (☐, ☐)

B1 You need CM 50.

Design your own island.

It could be a different pirate island.

It could be a holiday island.

- **a** Put 10 places or features on your island.
- **b** Write their co-ordinates.

Remember to draw them where 2 lines cross.

C1 Write the list of co-ordinates for the letters that spell your name.

C2 Use co-ordinates to write a message for a friend.

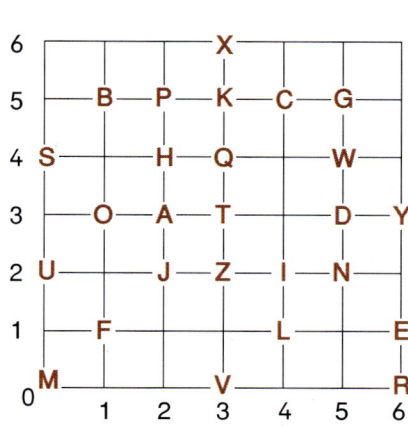

SS5 Position and direction

SS5.3 Describing and following directions

Key idea | We can use co-ordinates and compass directions to describe a route.

A1 Look at the pirate island on IP 21 or CM 48.

Pretend you are at Blue Mountain.

Use the compass to help.

a Which direction is Ashak Rainforest?

b Which direction is Hangman's Rock?

A2 Write down directions from

a Thunder Volcano to The Red Pig,

b Snake Swamp to Blue Mountain,

c Carib Village to Galleon Lake,

d Zantu Rainforest to the bridge,

e Blue Mountain to Hangman's Rock,

f Pirate Camp to Blue Mountain,

g Smugglers' Island to Sunken Treasure,

h The Red Pig to Eagle Rock.

B1 You need CM 48.

There is buried treasure under the Jolly Roger flag at (6, 7).

Pirate Pete from The Red Pig needs an easy route that passes landmarks he can spot on the way.

- **a** Use CM 48 to draw a route to lead him to the treasure.
- **b** Write down directions for Pete using co-ordinates and points of the compass.
- **c** Write him a list of the co-ordinates of the landmarks he will pass.

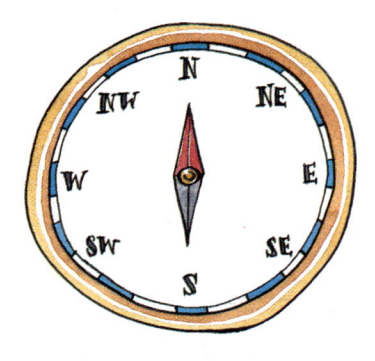

C1
- **a** Hide some treasure on the map.
- **b** Choose a starting place.
- **c** Write directions for a route that visits at least 3 other places on the way to the treasure.
- **d** Ask a friend to try it.

> Pirate Camp to Snake Swamp is not an exact NW direction. You could say 'roughly NW' or N then W.

Key idea We can use co-ordinates and compass directions to describe a route.

SS5 Position and direction

SS6.1 Measuring angles in degrees

| Key idea | A whole turn is 360°. A quarter turn, or right angle, is 90°. |

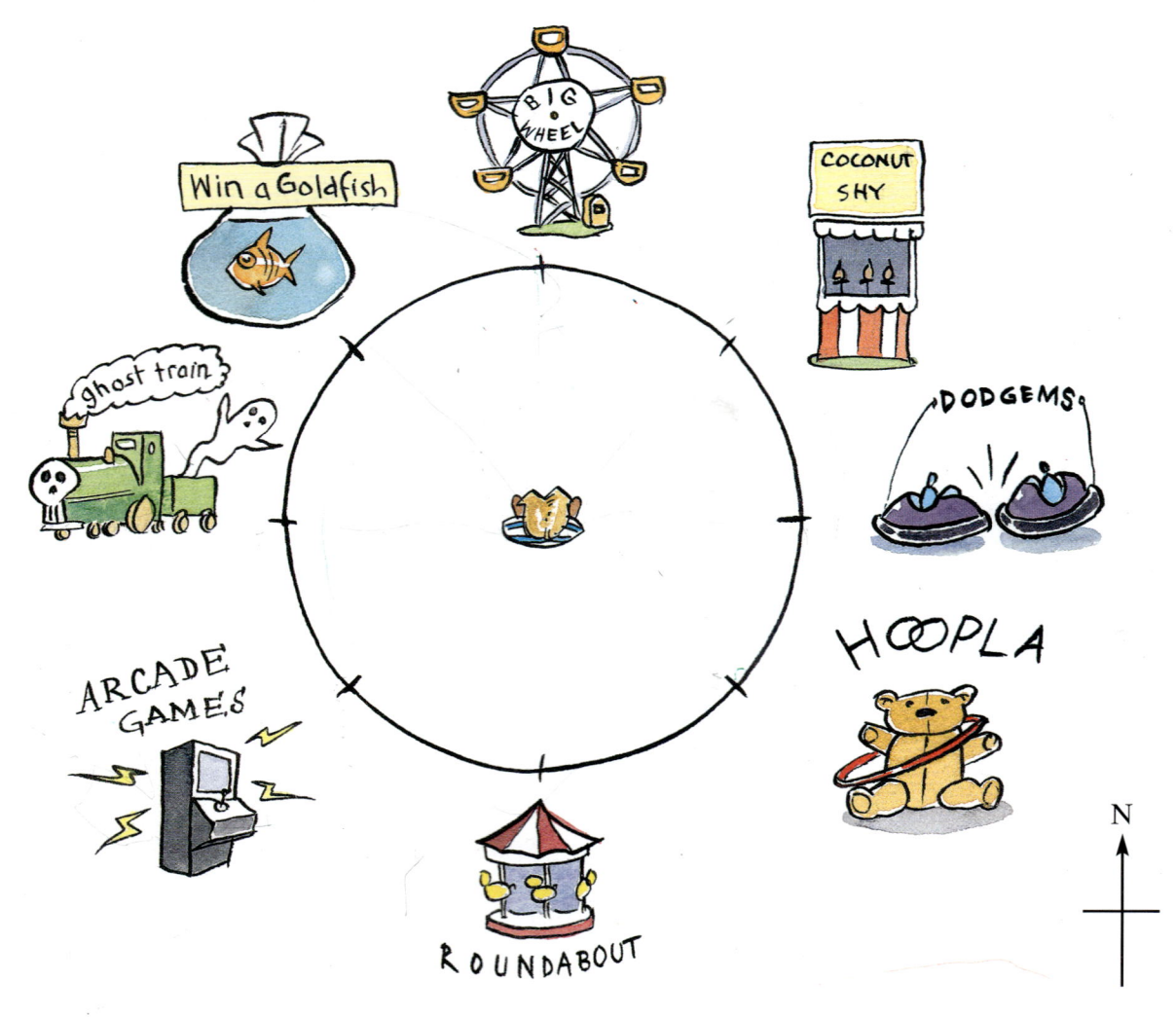

A1 Jack is at the fair. He is looking at the attractions.

Write what he will see if he faces the big wheel and then turns clockwise:

- **a** 90°
- **b** 180°
- **c** 45°

A2 How far will he turn if he turns:

- **a** anti-clockwise from 'Win a goldfish' to the ghost train?
- **b** clockwise from the hoopla to the arcade games?
- **c** anti-clockwise from the coconut shy to the arcade machines?

B1 Look at the picture on page 54. Copy and complete this table to show what Jack sees after he turns from his starting place.

	Start	Turn	End
1	Hoopla	clockwise 45°	Roundabout
2	Roundabout	anti-clockwise 90°	
3	Win a goldfish	clockwise 180°	
4	Coconut shy	clockwise 45°	
5	Ghost train	anti-clockwise 180°	
6	Arcade games	anti-clockwise one right angle	
7	Big wheel	clockwise 360°	

B2 Copy and complete this table, filling in any missing details.

	Start	Turn	End
1	Hoopla		Dodgems
2		clockwise three right angles	Win a goldfish
3	Coconut shy	clockwise 180°	
4	Big wheel		Dodgems
5		anti-clockwise 45°	Ghost train

B3 The big wheel is at the north end of the fairground.

In which direction is each of these attractions?

a Ghost train **b** Hoopla

c Roundabout **d** Win a goldfish

B4 If Jack faced NW and turned 90° clockwise, what would he see?

C1 If Jack faced SE and turned 45° anti-clockwise, what would he see?

C2 If Jack faced the dodgems, turned 180° clockwise and then 45° anti-clockwise, what would he be facing?

C3 Make up some similar questions for your partner to answer.

Key idea A whole turn is 360°. A quarter turn, or right angle, is 90°.

SS6 Movement and angle

SS6.4 Making and measuring turns

> **Key idea** An angle is a measure of turn.

A1 What angle has the hour hand turned through on each of these clocks?

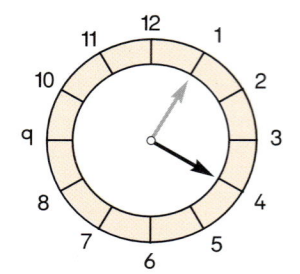

From 1 o'clock to 4 o'clock

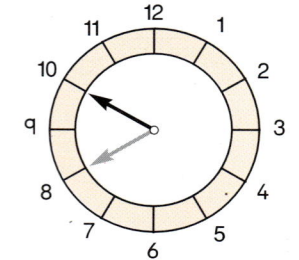

From 8 o'clock to 10 o'clock

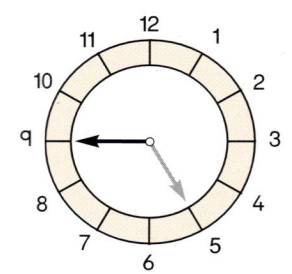

From 5 o'clock to 9 o'clock

B1 Do CM 54.

B2 On Monday the weather vane shows the wind blowing from the north.

On Tuesday the wind has changed direction.

It is now blowing from the north-west.

a How many degrees has it turned through?

On Wednesday it blows from the east.

b How many degrees did it turn through between Tuesday and Wednesday?

C1 The temperature control on a shower has 6 settings. 0 is cold and 5 is the hottest.

Work out how many degrees the control turns as it is moved from:

a 0 to 1   **b** 1 to 4   **c** 4 to 2

d 0 to 5   **e** 5 to 1

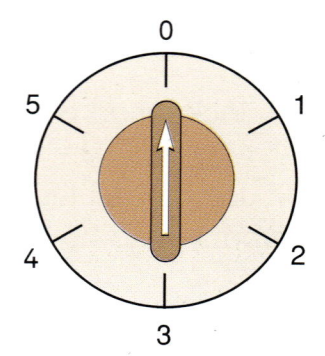

C2 Investigate the angles between each position for controls with 5, 10 or more settings.

56   SS6 Movement and angle

D1.1 Tallying

Key idea	We group tally marks in 5s to make them easier to count.

B1

Work with a partner.
You need 2 dice and CM 55.

Investigate which total score is the most common when you throw 2 dice.

- **a** On CM 55, make a list of all the totals you can make.
- **b** Roll the 2 dice 50 times and make a tally for each total.
- **c** What do you notice?
- **d** Try to explain why your most common total has appeared so often.

C1 You need a reading book.

Investigate what is the most common word in your reading book.

- **a** Choose 5 words that you think are used often.
- **b** Draw a tally chart in your book.
- **c** Choose any 5 pages.
  Read them and make a tally of your words.
- **d** Write about what you find.
- **e** What happens if you choose 10 pages for tallying?

HD1 Using tally charts, frequency tables and pictograms

HD1.2 Making pictograms

> **Key idea** We can use picture symbols to represent more than 1 unit.

★1

KEY:
- Angelfish
- Lion fish
- Clownfish
- Flying fox fish

You need CM 56.

a Make a pictogram showing how many of each kind of fish.

Use a symbol that represents 2 fish.

b Use your pictogram to find the missing information.

_____ is the least common fish.

There are ☐ more clown fish than lion fish.

There are ☐ times as many angelfish as flying fox fish.

C1 You need CM 56.

name of fish	number of fish
violet soldier	9
peacock rock cod	3
convict surgeon	24
blue fin jack	18
black footed clown	42
bird wrasse	54
two spot red snapper	45
reef lizard	15

a Look at the table. Make a pictogram.

b Write at least 4 sentences about the data.

For example:

There are 3 times as many violet soldiers as peacock rock cod.

Remember the key. How many fish does your symbol represent?

HD1.3 Using charts and tables

> **Key idea**: To solve a problem, we choose the information we need from tables or charts.

★1 Primesh and Amy are helpers at the snack shop this week.

Copy and complete.

a The most popular snack was _____.

b The least popular snack was _____.

c They sold ☐ items.

Snack shop sales Monday — Total sold 53
(bar chart: buns, brownies, raisins, fruit, drink)

"How much do we need for tomorrow?"

★2 Help Primesh solve his problem.

a Write what else you can find out from the chart.

b Sales on Tuesday are usually the same as on Monday.
How much do Primesh and Amy need for Tuesday?

Use a table for your answers to b.

HD1 Using tally charts, frequency tables and pictograms

A1 Class 4 is spending a week at High Cliffs Activity Centre.

One group does a survey of what activities people want to try.

Each child chooses 2 favourite activities.

They give the information to the staff in a pictogram.

Our favourite activities

archery	☺ ☺ ☾
climbing	☺ ☺ ☺ ☺
assault course	☺ ☺ ☺ ☺ ☺ ☺ ☺
grass tobogganing	☺ ☺ ☺ ☺
zip wire	☺ ☺ ☺ ☺ ☺ ☾
canoeing	☺ ☺ ☺ ☺ ☺

☺ represents 2 children

a Which 2 activities are most popular?

b How many children want to try the zip wire?

c How many more children chose the assault course than archery?

d Why do you think there are only a few children who want to try archery?

B1 It's Monday breakfast time at High Cliffs Activity Centre.

There's a problem – nearly everyone in class 4 has left their scrambled eggs.

So at supper, the cook does a survey.

He makes a mark for each way each child likes eggs cooked.

How children like their eggs

boiled	|||| |||| |||| |||| ||
scrambled	|||
poached	|||| |||| ||||	
fried	|||| |||| |||| |||| ||||	
omelette	|||| |||| ||||

There are 29 children in class 4

How do you think the cook should cook the eggs on Tuesday? Explain why.

HD1 Using tally charts, frequency tables and pictograms

B2 The centre staff want to get some different animals.

To help them decide which group of animals to get they carried out a survey.

They kept records of how many visits children made on one day to the animals they already have.

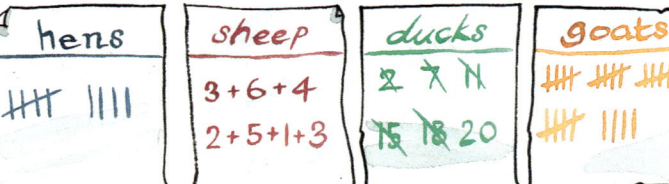

hens	sheep	ducks	goats	Pigs
﷽ IIII	3+6+4 2+5+1+3	2 7 N 15 18 20	﷽ ﷽ ﷽ ﷽ IIII	5+2+4 +4+4+ 3+5+6

a How many visits did the animals have in total?

b How many visits did the hens and ducks have?

c Which was the most popular animal? By how much?

d Help the staff decide which new animal to get.
Use information from the records to explain your suggestion.

C1 Mrs Makeithappen, the manager, needs a team leader for every 8 children.

She has a pictogram showing the numbers of children at the centre last week.

Monday	👤👤👤👤👤👤👤
Tuesday	👤👤👤👤👤
Wednesday	👤👤👤👤👤👤👤👤
Thursday	👤👤👤👤👤👤👤
Friday	👤👤👤👤👤👤👤👤
Saturday	👤👤👤👤👤👤👤👤👤
Sunday	👤👤👤👤👤👤👤👤👤👤

👤 represents 5 children

a How many children were at the centre on each day?

b Suggest how many leaders she needs to organise for next week.
Explain your reasoning.

Key idea To solve a problem, we choose the information we need from tables or charts.

HD1 Using tally charts, frequency tables and pictograms

HD2.1 Reading bar charts

| Key idea | The numbers on the vertical axis on a bar chart may be multiples of 2 or 5 or … |

A1 Mary comes from St Lucia. She loves the sunshine.

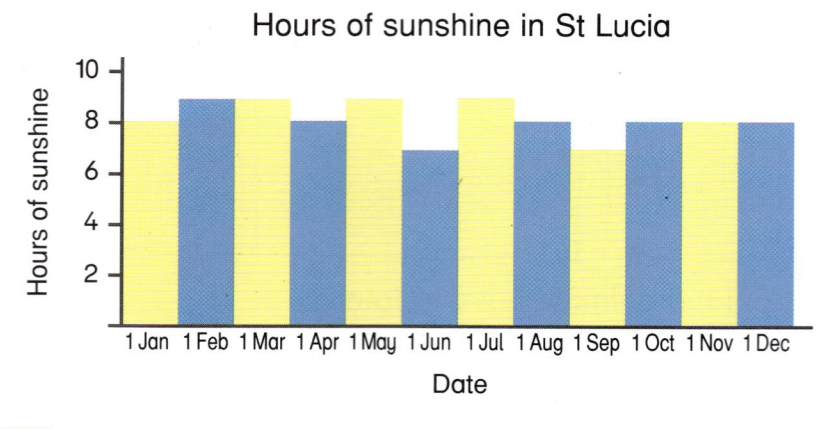

Hours of sunshine in St Lucia

a Which months began with the sunniest days?

b Which months began with the least sunny days?

c How many hours of sunshine did Mary enjoy on 1 November?

A2 Ahmed lives in the city of Cairo in Egypt. He enjoys times when it is cloudy.

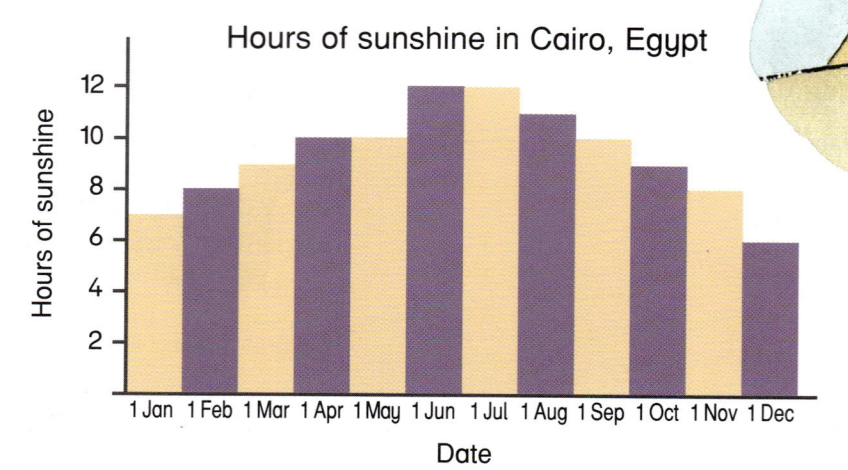

Hours of sunshine in Cairo, Egypt

a Which day had 11 hours of sunshine?

b Which days had less sunshine than 1 February?

c Which month started with the cloudiest day?

62 HD2 Using bar charts

B1 Work with a partner.

Look at the bar charts on page 62.

a Was there more sunshine in St Lucia or in Cairo on 1 May?

b Which place had less sunshine on 1 January?

c When and where do you think was the sunniest time of the whole year?

d Talk to your partner about the pattern of sunshine hours at the beginning of each month over the year in each place. Write about each pattern.

B2 This bar chart shows different temperatures around the world on 1 November.

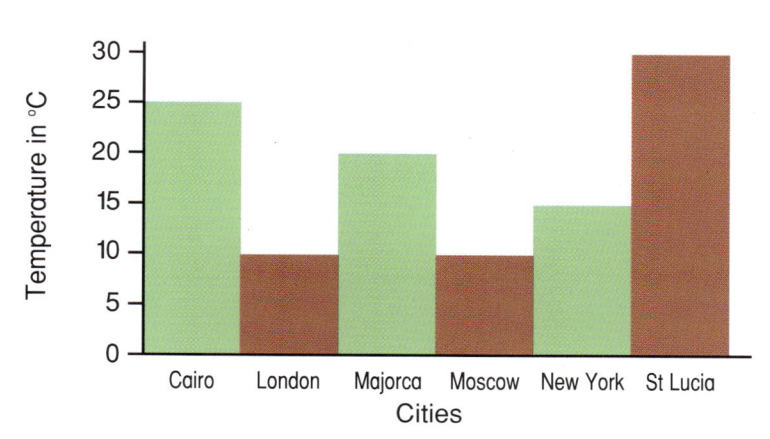

a List the temperatures in St Lucia, Cairo, Moscow and London.

b Make up 3 questions to ask about the bar chart.

You need 2 partners, CM 59 and a newspaper with a weather report.

C1 **a** Find a table showing the weather in different places in the UK. Choose 2 sets of data from it.

b For each set of data
- make a frequency table
- draw a bar chart on CM 59

First decide how to label the divisions on the vertical axis.

C2 **a** For each set of data in C1, produce bar charts with different divisions on the vertical axis.

b Discuss the charts, then write which you think is best and why.

| Key idea | The numbers on the vertical axis on a bar chart may be multiples of 2 or 5 or ... |

HD2 Using bar charts

HD2.3 Interpreting bar charts

| **Key idea** | We must look at the divisions on the axes of a bar chart carefully to find how many units each division represents. |

★1 Make a table of readings for each bar chart.

a How many in class 4 think books are brilliant?

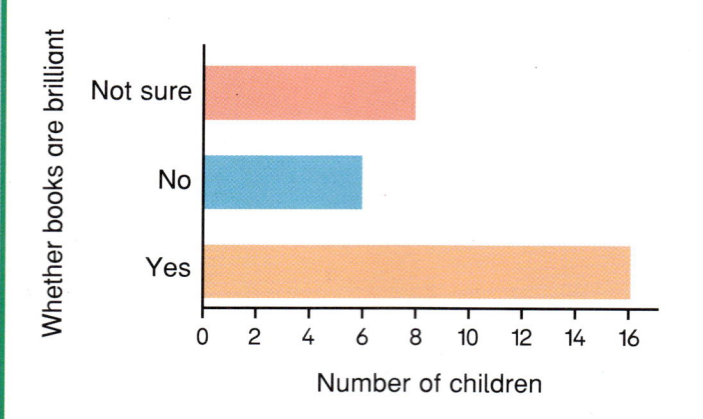

b How many children read books mostly from school, or home or the library?

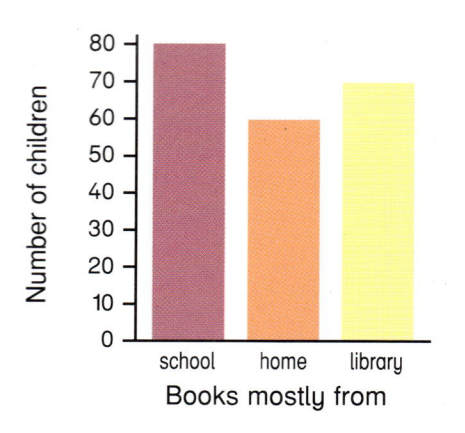

A1 Make a table of readings for each bar chart.

a How many children like fact, story, poetry or picture books best?

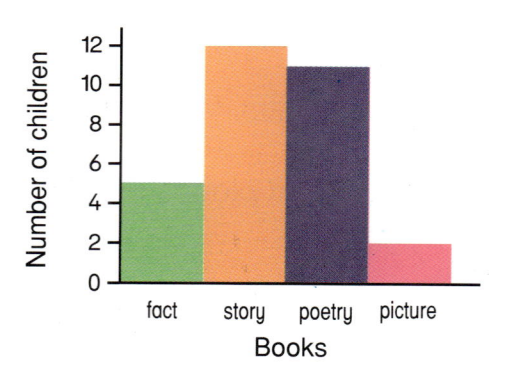

b How many children in year 4 read comics?

c Would children in the school like a book as a present?

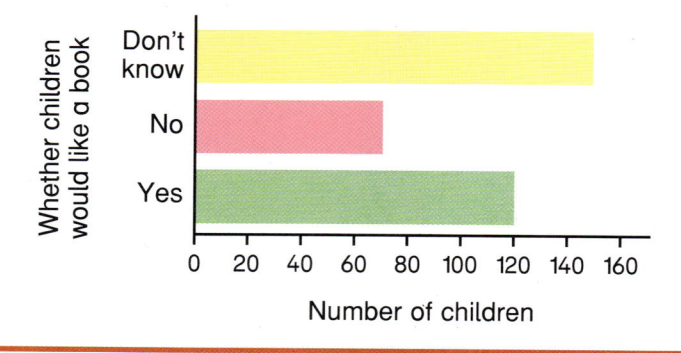

d What kind of poem do we like in class 4?

64   HD2 Using bar charts

A2

Challenge: How many vowels can you find in one paragraph?

This bit's got lots of vowels — I wonder how many?

This is what they found.

The number of vowels we found in one paragraph

a) Which was the least common vowel?

b) Which vowel appeared 35 times?

c) How many vowels did the children count altogether?

d) Which vowel appeared most frequently? Can you think of a reason for this?

e) Try to estimate how many words there were in the paragraph.

B1

a) In which month did St Lucia have the most rain?

b) How many centimetres of rain fell in June?

c) Did any months have the same amount of rainfall?

d) What is the difference between rainfall amounts in March and September?

Centimetres of rainfall in St Lucia

Jan 15, Feb 10, Mar 10, Apr 9, May 15, Jun 21, Jul 25, Aug 26, Sept 25, Oct 24, Nov 21, Dec 20

HD2 Using bar charts

B2

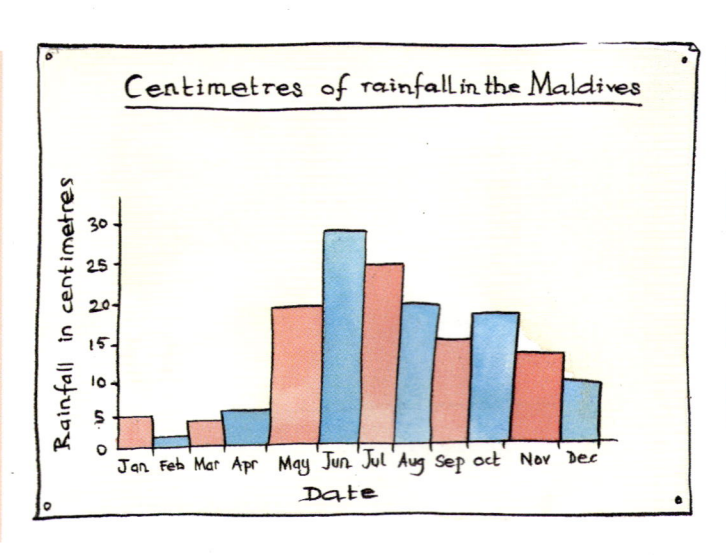

Centimetres of rainfall in the Maldives

(bar chart: Rainfall in centimetres vs Date, Jan–Dec)

a In which month did most rain fall in the Maldives?

b How much more rain fell in July than in December?

c Which is the driest month?

d How much rain fell in April?

C1

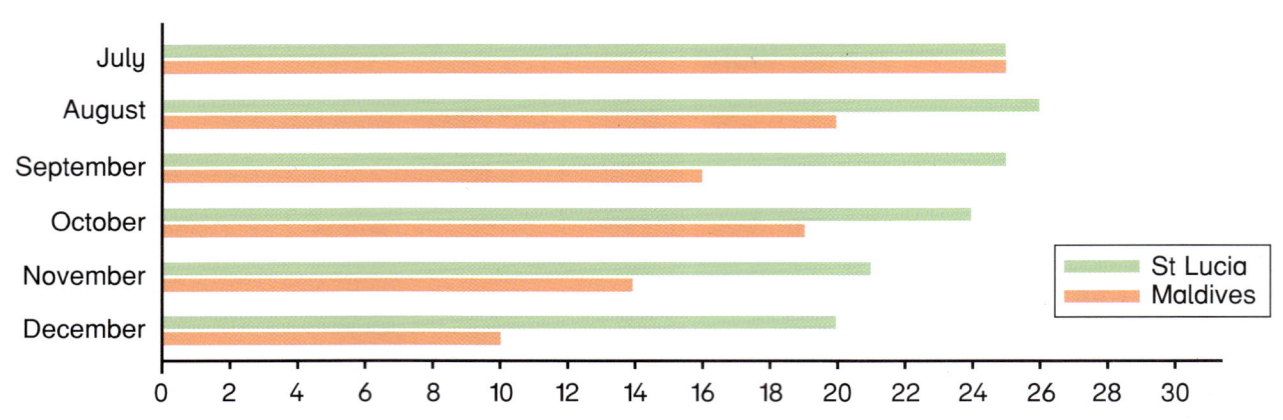

(horizontal bar chart comparing rainfall in St Lucia and Maldives from July to December, scale 0–30)

a How much more rain fell in August in St Lucia than in the Maldives?

b Are there any months when both places had the same rainfall?

c Is there more rainfall in St Lucia or in the Maldives?

C2 This chart shows how many people visited a dolphin attraction in St Lucia in one week.

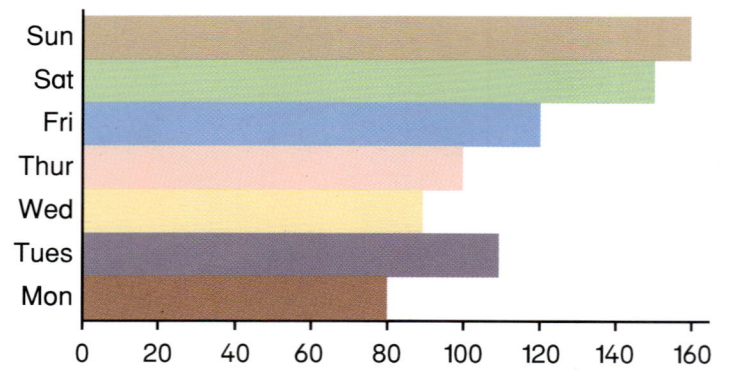

(horizontal bar chart showing visitors Mon–Sun, scale 0–160)

Write 5 questions about the data for a friend to answer.

| Key idea | We must look at the divisions on the axes of a bar chart carefully to find how many units each division represents. |

HD2 Using bar charts

D3.1 Venn diagrams

| Key idea | Items in the overlapping set match 2 ways of sorting. |

★1 You need a partner, 2 rings, these labels and these shapes.

`triangles`   `yellow shapes`

a Make this Venn diagram with your rings and labels.

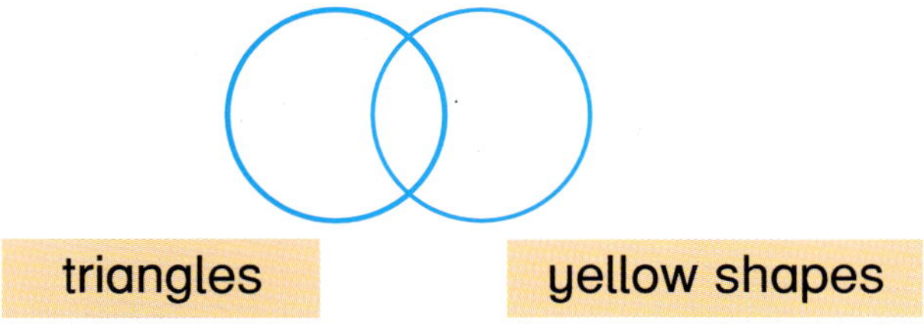

`triangles`   `yellow shapes`

b Sort your shapes.

c Draw a Venn diagram of how you sorted them.

d Which shapes are triangles and not yellow?

A1 You need CM 60.

Look at IP 24. There are children making music.

a Use one of the Venn diagrams to sort their instruments into:
- instruments made of metal,
- instruments that you blow.

b List the instruments that are blown and are not made of metal.

c Which of the instruments that you strike are not made of metal?

Use a Venn diagram.

HD3 Venn and Carroll diagrams

A2 Draw a larger copy of this Venn diagram (or use CM 60).

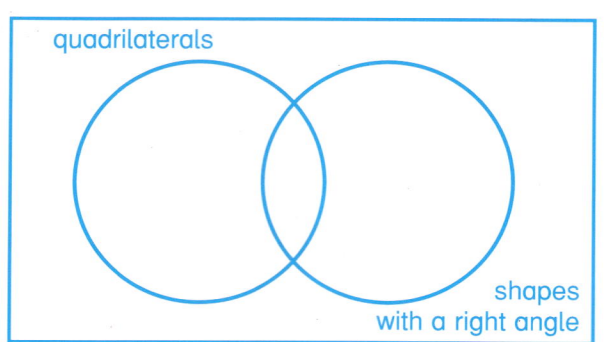

Flat shapes — quadrilaterals / shapes with a right angle

A quadrilateral has 4 straight sides.

You need some flat shapes.

a Sort your shapes.

- Think which ones belong in each circle.
  Draw them on your diagram.
- Find a shape that does not belong in either circle.
  Draw it on your diagram.

b Choose a shape from your diagram.

- Write its name.
- Why does it belong where you drew it?

B1

Flat shapes — A / B with a right angle

a Look at the way the shapes have been sorted.

A is the set of _____ .

b Describe the shape in the overlapping set.

c Describe where these shapes go on the diagram.

68   HD3 Venn and Carroll diagrams   CM 60

C1 **a** Draw larger copies of these Venn diagrams (or use CM 60).

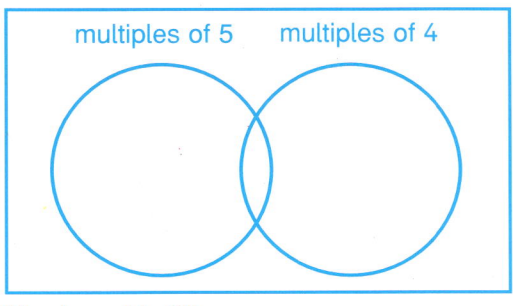

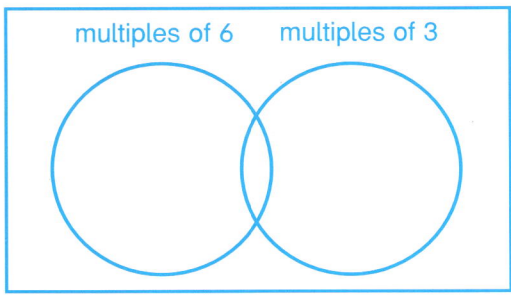

multiples of 5   multiples of 4

Numbers 1 to 20

multiples of 6   multiples of 3

Numbers 1 to 20

Use each diagram to sort these numbers:

1 2 3 4 5 6 7 8 9 10 11 12 13 14 15 16 17 18 19 20

b Copy and complete these statements:

☐ is a multiple of 4 and a multiple of 5.

☐, ☐, ☐ are multiples of 3 but not multiples of 6.

c Look at your diagram of multiples of 6 and 3.

- Check that one part is empty.
- Draw a different way to sort the numbers so that part of the Venn diagram is empty.

C2 Make up your own Venn diagram for sorting numbers.

- Think of 2 ways to sort.
- Choose 10 numbers to put on your diagram.
- Try and pick numbers for all parts of the diagram.

What shall I choose? Odds, evens, multiples, positives, negatives...

Key idea Items in the overlapping set match 2 ways of sorting.

HD3 Venn and Carroll diagrams

HD3.2 Carroll diagrams

> **Key idea** We must look at the labels at the top of each column and at the side of each row before sorting.

B1 Look at the diagram.

	divisible by 5	not divisible by 5
even	50 30	24 48
not even	35 45	49 27

a ☐ and ☐ are even and divisible by 5.

b ☐ and ☐ are even but not divisible by 5.

c ☐ and ☐ are not even but are divisible by 5.

d ☐ and ☐ are not even and not divisible by 5.

e Think of two more numbers for each part of the diagram.

B2 Look at this diagram carefully.

	has at least one line of symmetry	has no lines of symmetry
has 4 sides	1	2
does not have 4 sides	3	4

Where would these 4 shapes fit on the diagram: box 1, 2, 3 or 4?

a   b   c   d

C1 Look at the sports represented on this diagram.

	ball	no ball
net	1 tennis football	3 badminton ice hockey
no net	2 rounders rugby	4 darts running

a Why are football and rugby in different areas of the diagram?

b Where would you put cricket, basketball, netball, fencing?

c Change 'ball' to 'bat'? Draw a new Carroll diagram to show what happens.

D3.3 Interpreting sorting diagrams

> **Key idea** We can use different sorting diagrams to organise data.

★1 **Breakfast at the Browns**

	orange juice	no orange juice
toast	Mrs Brown, Connor	Ryan, Jake
no toast	Tom	Rebecca

Who has **a** toast and orange juice? **b** no toast and no orange juice?

A1 Look at the Carroll diagram in ★1.

a Who does not have orange juice? **b** Who does not have toast?

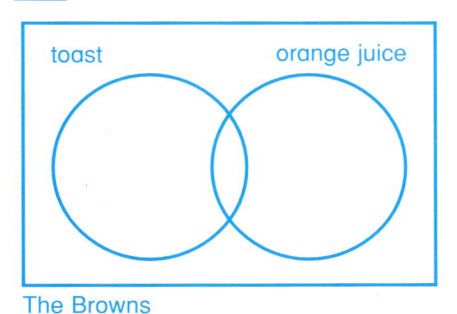

A2 **a** Copy this Venn diagram and put in the data from ★1.

b Whose name does not belong in the circles? Why?

(Venn diagram: toast ∩ orange juice — The Browns)

B1

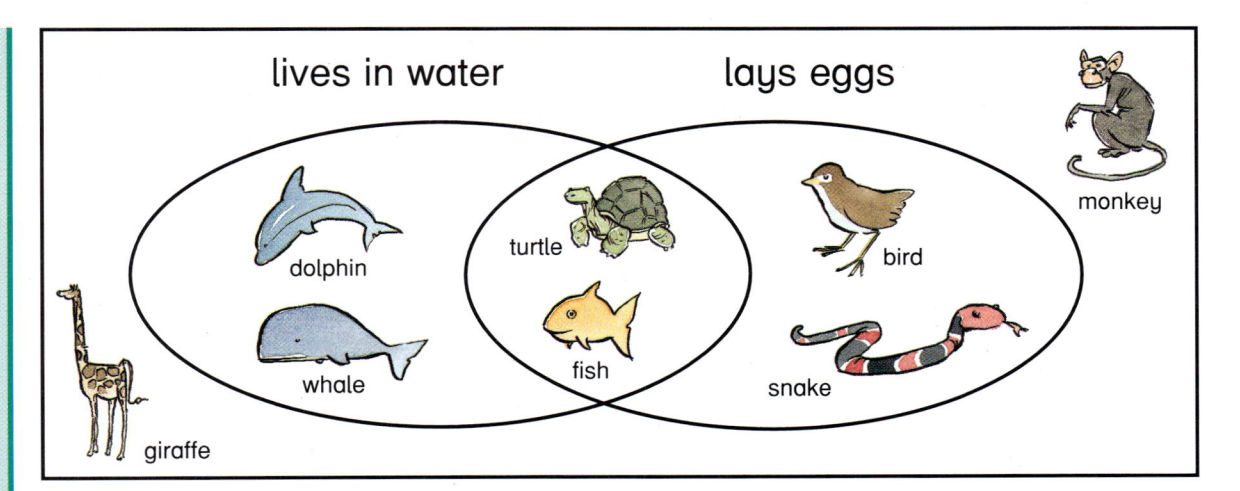

(Venn diagram: lives in water / lays eggs)
- lives in water only: dolphin, whale
- both: turtle, fish
- lays eggs only: bird, snake
- outside: giraffe, monkey

Copy and complete this Carroll diagram, using the information from the Venn diagram.

	lives in water	does not live in water
lays eggs		
does not lay eggs		

HD3 Venn and Carroll diagrams

B2

a Look at the picture.

Can you spot some insects?

Are there creatures that can fly?

Check using information from a book or a computer if you are not sure.

b Draw a diagram to sort the creatures into:

- ones that can fly and ones that cannot fly,
- ones that are insects and ones that are not insects.

You can choose which kind of diagram to use.

C1 Add some more creatures to your diagram for B2.

C2 Work with a partner.

a Discuss which would be the best diagram to show the answer to this sorting question:

- Do all brightly coloured insects eat parts of plants?

b Repeat **a** for your own sorting questions.

Key idea We can use different sorting diagrams to organise data.

HD3 Venn and Carroll diagrams